1

Summary

ƵO|

Copywriting

The aim of this book is to explain to the reader how copywriting can bring innumerable advantages to sellers.

If you have a business or an e-commerce site and you want to give a certain boost to sales, a writing job that best reviews the articles you sell is fundamental, especially on the web.

The market has changed and a good review, perhaps with a strongly persuasive and emotional edge, can make inroads among the readers, bringing them to the purchase.

In this book, therefore, we will focus on defining what copywriting is, what are the most popular techniques for successful writing, the role of SEO copywriting, nowadays essential in the era of the internet and social networks.

We will examine how the persuasive and emotional component plays in the current state of things a role increasingly determined in the eyes of the target audience.

However, the logical, informative and rational component must never be lacking so that you, as a writer, can be as reliable as possible and not just a salesman.

We will then analyze the barriers that the copywriter has the task of removing, in order to conclude a transaction, what an entrepreneur who hires a copywriter must judge and what are the possible job opportunities for this profession that, unlike many others, does not have a path clear and established but a myriad of paths, one distinct from the other.

In the text, then, there will be a whole series of useful tips on how to write a highly sales-oriented text. Enjoy the reading!

What is copywriting?

In terms of definition, copywriting should be interpreted as the art of knowing how to write well, sometimes informative, sometimes descriptive and, more and more often, as it has been since the boom in advertising, emotional and persuasive.

The target? Ensure conversion. A conversion that, especially in the web world, is represented by the conclusion of a purchase on an e-commerce site, perhaps following the reading of a nice product review written by you, a particularly brilliant copywriter, or a lead that can be subscribing to a newsletter, filling in a contact form and so on.

Each of these goals requires a style of communication that is also appropriate to the type of medium you write about.

Copywriting: origins

The term *copywriting* dates back to the nineteenth century and is specifically related to the journalistic world.

In the editorial offices of the most authoritative newspapers, the figure of the copywriter dealt with drawing up announcements of all kinds.

Subsequently, the advertising media boom, first in print and then on radio and TV, totally changed the cards on the table.

In fact, copywriting work was increasingly associated with advertising.

Contributing as a protagonist to the creation of a successful advertising campaign, starting from the creation of slogans to promote the product, were the main work activities for the copywriter, before the advent of the web.

Then, the success of digital marketing has radically changed his duties. So much so that in addition to the professionals who still work in tandem with the art director, who specializes in graphics, there are more and more freelancers covering the multiple textual aspects of the content put online:

think for example of the texts for social networks, to corporate blogs where product reviews need to be structured for SEO, so that they are attractive to the various search engines, so that Internet users can find the relevant information.

In short, at present copywriting is an integral part of internet communication.

Knowing how to communicate the message of a corporate brand, using the right words, the appropriate vocabulary and the specific SEO oriented writing technique are requirements that only a few possess.

This is why companies are increasingly looking for highly specialized figures in the world of the business writer.

And perhaps this research should be based on even more selective criteria, given that unfortunately in an increasingly more competitive market like today, many companies tend to rely on those who ask for lower compensation.

This, as we will explain later, is a huge mistake. There are those who write and those who write well. And to those who write well, merit must also be paid to the economy.

Most effective techniques

Which sales-oriented writing techniques can be considered the best? Giving a dry answer is always complicated.

However, a premise must be made about the copywriting activity. As a business writer, you have a dual task: to write well texts and announcements that, first of all must be noticed by the audience of reference.

Secondly, the target you want to return to must appreciate the value of the content you have written. Finally, the company that has chosen you to translate the characteristics of its products into real benefits for customers must take advantage of your work.

An advantage that has many facets, namely increased sales, increased turnover, growth in the customer base, gains in leads and more.

Having said that this is a creative job, establishing guidance rules for copywriting is not easy at all.

Therefore we try. Here are the guidelines of the action range in this field.

· Target identification: to whom to communicate? Currently, the message is more and more frequently addressed to the niche.

So the more specific the niche is, the easier the copywriting text will go.

· The predominant feature of the product must emerge: in a commercial script, the creative, informative, descriptive, technical and persuasive components must never be lacking.

You skilled copywriter have the task of mixing them, arousing emotions and triggering sensations in just a few seconds.

To fully achieve this ambitious goal, you must be able to impress an indelible memory in the minds of readers.

All within a few moments.

The expressions you use in the content must be able to evoke images that no longer go away.

But remember that at the end of the work, what will emerge will be the main feature of the product. The details must be specified within the review, but you must be able to measure them with wisdom, because at the end of the reading, the target you are communicating with will be local and will have to remember first and foremost the fundamental aspect of the product.

This is the so-called principle of formulating a single creative idea, also known as USP (Unique Selling Proposition).

Summing up, based on a specific brief, the most important characteristic, decided upstream of the strategy, must come out.

· Zero contradictions: within a text with images or a simple promotional announcement, there is no room for contradictions.

Also because only if you present an excellently structured content, the reading will be as smooth and the decoding will appear more simple. All in full harmony with what the target is looking for.

Having made these clarifications, we review the most common business writing techniques, especially on the web.

Words Consistency

In an SEO oriented text, the keywords must be present in the title of a text, but also in the content of the announcement or article or review. Their use must be measured and the insertion in the text must take place in the most natural way possible, in order to avoid their over-optimization (ndr known as keyword stuffing) which, inevitably, involves a penalty on search engines.

It is good to combine the keywords with others, most often different, so that the content of the message is strengthened. We will go into this later when we define the

principles of SEO Copywriting.

Concreteness in writing style

Whether it is a review or a simple post, the concreteness in the writing style is essential to attract the greatest number of readers, in reference to a product.

Moreover, why should the consumer buy it? As a copywriter, it is up to you to explain it, using a concrete writing style.

Citing numerical data, explaining how to solve a problem, but also using metaphors, because strong images remain in the mind of the reader, they are the key to success in this field.

The Problem Technique

It is a very common copywriting technique, especially for what concerns tutorials. A question is posed to which many Internet users look for an answer.

Before explaining the solution to the problem, the goal is to involve as many readers as possible. Eye that the question asked should not be rhetorical, because if the reader already knows the solution, you seriously run the risk of making every effort vain.

The Alternative technique

Also known as the contrast technique, it is a very widespread scheme when writing with a strong sales orientation.

As an expert in the field, as a copywriter, you can give a question a concrete answer, as a primary solution, and an alternative, always valid. The same is true in the context of online sales.

To suggest the X product as a basic choice for a well defined target, and the product Y, as a valid option, is a rewarding system.

The important thing is to highlight every single advantage of both primary and secondary choice, but only after having highlighted the characteristics of the two articles. An action of this kind will ensure that you are targeting the target in order to be able to count on more probabilities of satisfying your needs in the best way.

Call to Action

We will discuss the call to action in more depth later on.

For now, we limit ourselves to saying that in the era of the Net, in closing any post, be it a landing page or a review or a commercial ad, the invitation to buy the product, to interact with the brand or signing up for a newsletter is increasingly fashionable.

Only with a highly emotional and persuasive writing technique can the reader be guided towards this step.

Starting from the invitation to action, as we have just highlighted, persuasive copywriting plays a crucial role.

It is not a type of writing for everyone, since there are precise rules to follow, certain analyzes to be carried out, especially in product reviews, and, above all, to use the appropriate vocabulary.

Target? Persuade the target audience of the goodness of a decision. The starting point of persuasive writing revolves around the analysis of the reader's desires. In fact, it is the needs of the target that move every single action.

The reader must be able to touch the product with the right words. Only if you are a skilled copywriter, will you be able to make every reader see the article reviewed live. A persuasive style of writing must touch emotions.

It is true that sometimes the consumer buys on impulse. However, nowadays, the world has changed: in fact there are a whole series of categories, such as food and drink, telephony, IT, where customers are very prepared and want to know what they buy, starting from the information they already have.

As a well-traveled business writer you will need to be able to touch the right ropes.

And to achieve this ambitious and challenging goal, there are rules in the field of persuasive coypwriting that are often worth sticking to.

In detail:

Preferring narration to description is the first step that a copywriter must consider, when it aims to convince readers of buying a product.

The cancellation of negative sentences must be seen in this sense. "No" and "no" should appear as little as possible.

Eye to the beginning and end of the text: they are the focal points of what you put black on white. Readers on the web initially make a quick read. What matters in any post is the beginning.

It is essential that it is smooth. Only in this way can the attention of the reader be attracted.

The same applies to the lock which must leave something, that is to say, what is special about that product, what distinguishes it from its competitors and why it is worth having. All, of course, before the call to action.

In the middle of the review, regardless of the length, I look at the use of keywords and bold. The attention of the reader is also attracted in this way.

The call to action gives the persuasive cut. Those who read should be guided towards the goal that, as already indicated, can be the purchase of a product, the click on a link, the insertion of one's own e-mail address for a newsletter. A direct style like an arrow and the impression of an urgent character are the determining factors for making inroads into the hearts of readers.

At the center there are always readers: speaking with their language is the easiest way to reach any goal.

You don't have to just sell

Persuasive copywriting, as we have pointed out, means inducing the potential customer to make the purchase or internet user on duty to perform the classic call-to-action.

However, this does not mean selling at all costs.

A copywriting, whose only imprinting is that of selling, makes reading difficult in the long run, revealing itself to be tiring and in some respects unreliable.

If you use this style of writing, the end result turns out to be in fact counterproductive, since your reliability will be undermined.

Furthermore, the client you work with, be it a company or an e-commerce site, will never benefit from it. So, you'll also be playing future collaborations.

Aggressive business writing, whose techniques originate from direct marketing, does not reward in any way.

Little but sure.

Forcing people to take action against the consumer, wanting to capture the attention of those who visit that website, whatever the cost, rather than being an excellent copywriter, they will make you look like a door-to-door salesman (not even very good) also because, with online channels, that contact is missing, that direct approach with the customer that sometimes has the effect due to the conclusion of a transaction.

When writing, therefore, do not think of selling as the number one goal.
Think about what obstacles you need to remove, so that whoever reads you will find it interesting how much you write.

It is no longer as it was in the past, given that, especially thanks to the advent of the Internet, consumers are better prepared and a good slice of purchases, whether these products are at the supermarket, clothes, luxury cars, notebooks, smartphones, tablets, books, gourmet foods are discretionary in nature.

It is therefore impossible to oblige the customer to purchase, regardless of the style of writing that you adopt.
You will be able to induce him to purchase, but you will certainly not be able to force him.

This means that through persuasive copywriting techniques, you will capitalize on a pre-existing need, transforming it into a concrete action.

With the emotional cut you will give to the contents, you will have to create attractiveness towards the described or reviewed products, which the users, especially online, continually seek either because they have a particular problem and intend to solve it or to improve their lifestyle or sometimes for a simple whim.

To induce the customer to purchase, some of the questions you should ask yourself as a business writer are the following: why do many customers have an interest in that product, while others do not even consider them?

What stops the natural inclination to purchase numerous end-users?

Because on a website, many Internet users see different product categories, but then they never go to the cart page?

Basically, there are a whole series of obstacles and impediments that in part, since not everyone has a solution, can be removed with excellent copywriting work.

A persuasive and emotional connotation of an editorial content, be it a review or a simple post of advice, can be useful in making the buyer say yes and boost sales.

Your goal as a writer is primarily to identify these barriers that jeopardize the actions of those who read you and then proceed with their elimination.

On the other hand, copywriting is always concerned with sales that tend to rise when there are no objections in the minds of readers.

And it's up to you to wipe them away with messages that leave a measurable impression.

We therefore see in quick overview what these threats are to be removed.

Identification barrier

Anyone has a personal image that affects their modus operandi. Also during the purchase phase.

As a business writer, when you are reviewing a product, you have to ask yourself if a consumer like you can actually be interested in buying that product. Always ask yourself if what you wrote succeeds in capturing the attention of the reference audience and if the contents can have a connection with the target.

If yes, you worked well and removed the identification barrier. At least this is the first step, to be successful, because your words have convinced you.

Clarity barrier

The chances of being able to sell an article to the reader are 0% in the world of copwriting, when the latter does not understand what you have written. The savoir faire, the personal style, the elegance, the good gab, the presence are elements that come out in direct sales. In writing, the contents are important. Make sure the offer is clear. To all. The details of the article must then be understandable above all by the potential target. If what you wrote is clear to you, after a second (or why not, a third and a fourth rereading), it

means that you have worked well and that
you have removed the barrier of clarity.

Product identity barrier

The product you are writing about, must inevitably have a distinctive identity that makes it in fact unique compared to the many competitors. After writing the text, try replacing the name of the product in question with that of the most well-known competitor on the market. If the text does not run as smooth as oil, it means that you have worked well, because it has removed the barrier to the identity of the product. Otherwise, if the reading is out of tune, well ... it means that you have not been able to establish the identity of the product and that the end-user, reading your text, will not be able to recognize the actual advantages on why it is worth buying. As a persuasive writer, with an eye to sales, you must have the ability to transform all the main features of the product into advantages for the end customer.

Immediacy barrier

From the first lines you have to go straight to the point and explain why buying that product is good and urgent. Who reads you must have a clear picture of the benefits of the article. Rewarding those who immediately accept the offer or highlighting that only the last pieces are available from stock is often a winning strategy.

Review the text you have written. If you are convinced that the product is so beautiful to be bought urgently, well then you have worked optimally, because you managed to remove the barrier of immediacy.

Reliability barrier

Especially in a review, when you write you must appear in the eyes of those who read you credible and reliable. Words give excellent results only if all customer doubts are dispelled.

Eye, however, that there are no miracles in the promotional field.

Using amazing words to pump the product will not have the desired effect.

The quoted testimonials of those who have already tested the product, revealing themselves to be extremely satisfied, is the first step in having a transaction completed. The same applies to obtaining positive feedback from industry experts. The classic opinion leaders.

If you reread the text, you will be convinced that it is worth buying the product you reviewed, you did a good job and you have removed the reliability barrier

Barrier of involvement

A more immersive reality makes readers and therefore the target audience of the product you are describing more involved.

Inciting their involvement through a checklist or through a quiz is now more and more fashionable, especially on social pages.

It is up to you as a copywriting expert to put the words down to make the offer more attractive. Why is it that today the most is filling in a form or inserting photos, videos, animations, audio?

Simply because they facilitate the activation of the senses.

A well-coordinated work, in this respect, the need for a close collaboration between the copywriter and the art director.

If in the end the work of which you have been the protagonist seems particularly beautiful to you, it means that you have done an excellent job, because you have removed the barrier of involvement.

Acceptability barrier

The need to be satisfied is to see if the emotional needs you mentioned in the post are particularly in line with those of the target audience. The product must be presented in a very pleasant way. This means that to the persuasive component it is necessary to place side by side of things also the logical, rational one. Only in this way, the text you drafted will not be too commercial.

If you were able to remove the barrier of acceptability, you will only know it over time. Therefore, some factors will prove to be very useful. For example, the entrepreneur you work with will be able to see his audience not as an indistinct and faceless audience, but as a clearly defined target, made up of highly satisfied individuals.

Your readers will see your calls to action particularly meaningfully.

In the long term, those who have worked with you will have long-term contacts with the possibility of repurchase. This means that he will probably want to work with you again, to get you to review more products or maybe he will report you to friends, if they specialize in other businesses.

The world of copywriting also relies heavily on word of mouth.

Moreover, in the face of positive results, as a business writer you will be increasingly able to develop an increasingly realistic approach when you write to sell. And if you're good at that, you might even be able to get around and break the writing rules, creating new ones from scratch.

But this ability is the prerogative of very few. White flies.

The common denominator of these operations of removal of the various barriers consists in fact in being able to package a message tailored to each reader, so that those emotions grow in him that, once they create a concrete need for the product you splendidly reviewed, will induce him to buy it.

SEO Copywriting

On the subject of copywriting, reference has been made to the term SEO. What is the difference between copywriting and SEO copywriting?

Basically, copywriting must be understood as the art of knowing how to structure informative, descriptive contents characterized by a strong emotional and persuasive connotation; SEO copywriting, in addition to the aforementioned criteria, presupposes an optimized writing on search engines.

The internet in fact offers all businesses, indistinctly, numerous business opportunities. And SEO copywriting allows each company to be found by actual customers and potential customers both on Google and on various search engines. For this to happen, conditio sine qua non is the writing of authoritative, interesting, useful and pertinent texts with Internet users' searches. All SEO oriented.

From an SEO copywriting perspective, meta data should be used in a workmanlike manner. The same applies to the structuring of the contents. The keywords must be inserted in the title and present in the text. Only in this way, indexing will be at the highest levels. In commercial writing, more web-oriented, for an article to be attractive to search engines, H1, H2, meta description and keywords should be used with criteria.

The more the SEO rules, which we will shortly indicate, will be respected, the higher the ranking of the text on search engines. And for a company, this translates into a considerable advantage.

Three e-commerce sites sell that food processor that is so popular in recent times. One has only the description of the product, the other a simple review and, finally, the last one optimized on the web with an indication of the strengths and testimonies of those who bought the item and was highly satisfied.

What do you think has the best chance of appearing on the first page of Google? Clearly the last one, can't you find it too? In the face of large numbers, in the world of e-commerce, sell that product that appears on the first page of Google in a natural way. when the Internet users search for it by inserting only its name in the query, well... it is a very significant competitive advantage, as the company increases sales, collects money, frees up space in the warehouse and benefits in terms of turnover.

Do you understand that a role of primary importance must be attributed to SEO copywriting?

So here are the most relevant rules in the production of content on the web that a good SEO copywriter must take into consideration.

Title tags, meta descriptions, header tags, URLs and text must be optimized for search engines. This is possible only when, as a copywriter, you know the rules and secrets of business writing on the web in detail, Therefore ...

Title Tag

Of all the SEO factors, the Title tag is by far the most decisive. The title keyword must be placed at the beginning, next to the site name. The only exception to this rule is only the homepage, where the brand name must have the right relevance, just as if it were the keyword. For the other web pages it becomes crucial to insert the relevant keywords in a meaningful way: the name of the brand, however, should not be included at all. The reason for this strategy is that following the keyword with the brand name results in a reduction in the importance given by the title tag to the associated keyword.

Another gross error to keep clear of is the insertion of excess text within the title tag.

Its greater length corresponds to a clear division of the importance assigned to the different keywords in the text.

Meta description

It should always be valued, as it must best describe the web page that the visitor is about to read. Also in this, the call to action that invites you to click right there is very useful, unlike doing so on one of the other available results. In this way, the company that operates in e-commerce has the possibility of achieving one of the many objectives already mentioned several times. Although among these, the sale of a product is almost always the most important.

Header tags

Use in the text h1, h2, h3 tags. It is vitally important to make the reading more fluent: the header tags ensure that the paragraphs are not excessively long and that the information is not presented, in terms of character, in a flattened manner. Adopting header tags, especially for content of a certain length, is a wise decision. In relation to the rules for writing header tags, we immediately tell you that there are no definite ones. Their usefulness is to give a title to the paragraph or to the reference paragraph below.

Url Keyword Rich

Containing keywords is one of the essential requirements of web page URLs, given the importance that the Mountain View Colossus search engine attaches to this aspect. The keywords, and especially the primary one, must be present in the URL which, in turn, must be exploited precisely to give them considerable visibility. In this way, the positioning of the page will be even more natural.

Paragraphs

SEO copywriting has undergone an important change in recent years. Writing an over-optimized text from an SEO point of view, until a few years ago, allowed you to have more visibility on the web than the competition, for what concerns the use of those specific keywords. The result, however, is that this excessive optimization annoyed and not a little the Internet users.

Today, this principle has changed. When writing, the text must be designed not for the search engine, but for the reader.
Knowing how to enhance the title tag, meta description, header tags and paragraphs is the key to getting the right visibility online.

What about text and paragraphs at this point?

The text must respond perfectly to the title tag and the description, so that the reader does not be disappointed when accessing the web page from Google's SERP.

In the absence of this assumption, as a copywriter, you will not be clearly writing for the reader, but for the search engine.

And on this point, it is good that you immediately realize it when you start writing. The reason? The satisfaction of the reader is at the moment the main point that

Google takes into consideration. On this aspect, especially in recent years, progress has been truly remarkable. The merit must be assigned to updates to qualitative algorithms that return web pages to the internet user, more and more in line with her research questions. Basically, all those websites and web pages that best respond to the queries of those who surf the web are the winners.

The long form

Recently, one of the most popular topics in the field of copywriting is certainly the long form, also known as pillar article. What is it essentially? Specifically, it is a text rich in content that in some respects closely resembles a mini tutorial.

Have you ever tried to search on Google for "How to ..." and to find a mini guide, where you had to click on "Next" to view the individual steps from time to time?

Well, the long form is this but without the annoying chopping of the text into multiple pages.

A mini tutorial that fits into a single web page with the individual passages enumerated, one after the other. This is very widespread in the field of sales-oriented writing, but also in the field of IT-oriented websites or in generalist news blogs or in editorial magazines.

Ultimately, the underlying mission of the long form is to give you an excellent opportunity, namely to create a whole series of web pages that are positioned on the various search engines based on specific keywords. All without having to insert external links.

There is no ideal length that allows you to classify that text as a long form. However, the minimum presence of 2,500 words and 3 or 4 paragraphs is a prerequisite for developing a specific topic in depth. Each long form revolves around a central keyword and several secondary keywords.

Using an index in html format, to be placed under the title is a wise choice for a good construction of a long form of art. The underlying reason for this strategic choice, in fact, is to present in a concise way, through an easy navigation path, which points are analyzed in the mini guide, thus giving the reader immediately the possibility of knowing where to find the solution to his question.

Keyword research

In reference to business writing on the web, the topic of SEO copywriting represents the decisive phase, as the actual research intent, the various synonyms of the main keyword that Internet users could type online, all the features that present a association with the keyword, ie price, recipient, destination and, finally, all the relevant adverbs: how, where, how, when, why and so on. In this phase, as a copywriter, the search query expansion method will be decisive.

The structure to be followed will in fact be of a pyramid type: the keyword placed at the top, followed in rapid succession by secondary keywords based on the greater volume of traffic and all the semantic links that the internet user could type on the search engine.

Fortunately, in this process, you will be able to count on various tools that the world of the web puts at your disposal: Google Keyword Planner, Google Suggest, AnswerthePublic and Keyword Magic Tool are certainly the most competitive. The common denominator of these tools is the precise work focused primarily on the analysis of the primary keywords and only subsequently on the levels of competition and traffic volumes.

And in reference to the content to be structured, be it an article or a mini guide, what do you have to do as a sales-oriented commercial writer?

The keyword must be the basis of the article and is present in every paragraph, sub paragraph and under the title.

This means that you will need to use the largest possible number of variables in an organic and logical way, so that Internet users will find your content on search engines on one side and readers on the other hand to consider the article relevant to their query.

Conclusions

Here, therefore, are the tricks to keep in mind in the context of SEO copywriting.

· For the title, it is preferable to opt for the h1 tag

· For paragraphs, it is wise to adopt the h2 tag

· For the sub paragraphs, it is good to prefer the use of the h3 tag

· The keywords must be used in the most natural way possible, but in a manner consistent with what the title of the article and its contents indicate

· In order to avoid over-optimization, due to the continuous use of the same keywords, dosing the variables wisely makes the texts even better structured: singular, plural and synonyms of the keyword are always welcome

· Bold and italics are very useful, because they make the reading smoother. Moreover, since the contents immediately jump to the sight of the visitors, they have the possibility to find as soon as possible the information pertinent to their search

· Bulleted lists and numbered lists make the reading smoother

· In order for a text to be optimized on search engines, Google in the first place, with an ideal minimum length is 300 words

· Using internal links and external links is an excellent strategy: the important thing is that all the sources highlighted are consistent with the argument, authoritative as sources and useful to those who surf the Internet. The links must always be inserted on anchor text of a certain relevance.

· The use of meta tags is indispensable, so that Google and other search engines consider the text to be of a certain level

· The images eventually inserted in the text must be named using the keywords adopted in the contents. If in the event there were alternative fields, also in this case it is necessary to compile them. Particularly eye to the meta description. This is essentially the summary of what was written. It is important that the keywords, even in this situation, are always present.

Online Tools

If you want to do SEO Copywriting in Italian, there are a whole series of online tools available on the Net that can be extremely useful. These are basically tools that do textual analysis, but not only. In this paragraph, we will present them one by one in rapid tracking, in relation to what appears to be their primary function.

1. Identification of sources and definition of ideas: the creative process

This is the first phase of SEO Copywriting, where the work is basically scouting. Reason for which the consultation of the sources, aimed at identifying the statistics, the various points of view and the relevant case studies, is of primary importance for the definition of ideas, for the creation of the text and for the enrichment of contents. Two of the most competitive tools of all are Pocket (www.getpocket.com) and Feedly (www.feedly.com).

- Pocket: what it is and how it works

What is Pocket? In a nutshell, this is a valid online application to save articles to read them more calmly at a later time and to have all your interests at hand. Specifically, this content care tool allows you to start working on the right foot, since you can order ideas sensibly, critically evaluate selected cues and decide which ones to discard and which ones to use and then share them later . Pocket is one of the most successful tools in the field of SEO Copywriting due to its considerable practicality: first of all it ensures that you do not miss the links of all the articles, photos and videos you wish to consult later. In this way, in fact, the organization and productivity of your work will benefit.

The Pocket operation logic is simple and intuitive: once on the homepage, all you have to do is create an account by registering via e-mail or via Google. After that, immediate saving of articles, images and videos will be a breeze, since you can count on the appropriate button or on the Google Chrome bookmarklet, Safari, Firefox. Once you have selected the posts that you consider most noteworthy, these will be added to your personal list. Alternatively, Pocket offers you the possibility to insert the links also from within the application or in the web page called Save an item to Pocket. The possibility of tagging your links in the way that suits you best is really very convenient, since you will have a better organization from your side. The internal search, in this regard, allows you to more easily find the contents that, depending on your actual needs, can also have multiple tags. All editable and removable, of course. The Untagged items item is very useful because it allows you to consult all those contents, which were saved without inserting any tag.

Clearly, advanced features are not lacking. The links that have impressed you the most can be placed in the favorites, with the star mark. If you consider it appropriate, you can also put them in the archived (editor's note: Archive). Excellent Text to Speech (TTS) function that reads the article of interest in the language you set. In this way, you will be able to listen and collect the idea while you are busy with other matters.

The beauty of Pocket is that it works perfectly even off-line, since the contents can be read even when you are not connected.

The same applies to reading at a later time: in this case, you can select one of the two available fonts, enlarge or reduce the font and select one of the three colors for the layout. All the contents saved, therefore, with Pocket can be consulted even without being online. Connection, on the other hand, is an essential requirement for sharing content on social networks, such as Facebook and Twitter or via e-mail. In this last example, the item to be selected is Send to a friend: the recipient will see the link not only in his e-mail box, but, if he is a registered user, also in the Inbox of this very valid web-based service, clean in the interface and extremely user-friendly in terms of use.

Also for Recommendations, internet connection is essential. The beauty of Pocket is that over time it starts to know what your actual preferences are and to suggest which content is most relevant to you. In fact, when you write, you will lose less and less time in selecting sources. The most interesting ones, you can easily collect them in the Recommended section. Last thing to be specified about Recommendations is that you can save and tag content that is worth reading to you. Then it will clearly be up to you to decide whether to take inspiration from these sources in the sales-oriented online writing phase.

Another first-order advantage in using Pocket lies in teamwork. Still with the Send to a Friend function, you can insert content into the interface of the online application and send an e-mail message to add@getpocket.com. The contents entered will be sent to the list you have created. By adding the e-mail addresses of your team members from your personal profile options, you can easily work in groups, even remotely.

Summing up, Pocket is really the non plus ultra if you constantly look for ideas for your content and you don't always have time available for screening the sources. Ditto if you can't read on the fly. How many times having a look at the social pages or your favorite internet sites, did you happen to find really interesting contents, but that in that specific moment you could not consult? Well, Pocket solves your problem.

- Feedly: what it is and how it works

In the SEO copywriting branch, Feedly turns out to be a high-level tool, for the simple reason that it allows you to increase your knowledge and identify the essential points to share relevant topics, especially in the field of social media marketing and blogging. Select the sources with the utmost care: this is essentially the basic function of the aforementioned online service, in order to improve your work. The moment you consult content posted by other users and intend to use it, Feedly lets you name them or more precisely to address your sources with extreme precision. One of the most used systems in the field of source selection is the organization of content by project, where it focuses on customers. Specifically, each directory constitutes a project that contains the most suitable sources for the creation of new texts. Idem for the organization of content by theme, where folders are used to synthesize the themes for the development of a single project.

But the functions of this valuable resource certainly do not end here. Feedly turns out to be an excellent feed reader that, among other things, is one of the most appreciated by bloggers. The distinctive feature of this online service lies in the fact that thanks to RSS feeds it is not necessary to constantly follow your favorite blogs. The contents can be read easily in the feed reader.

Another interesting aspect of Feedly is the possibility of adding a blog. All you have to do is search from the appropriate bar or type in the URL and press enter. From the added blog box, you will see the preview of the last posted content. By clicking on the green cross, you will have completed the operations. The strength of Feedly lies in the possibility of defining in the read which content to publish on social networks and what to highlight later. For every post published on Feedly there are a whole series of valid blogging tools. This is also very useful for sales-oriented writing. As a business writer, in fact, you can highlight an interesting article for a project. If you then want to go deeper into it, perhaps to rework it, you can save it in the Saved for later folder. For sharing on social networks, nowadays more and more important to increase traffic on your client's website and, consequently, to give an impulse to his sales, if he also did e-commerce, you can take advantage of all the functions on the right side of the menu. The same is true for sending content to your contacts through an e-mail message. However, these functions are only available in the version of Feedly Pro (https://feedly.com/i/pro), the price currently amounts to 5.41 dollars a month.

So, to sum up, choosing Feedly as a working tool in the business writer branch is very practical both for a speech organizing discovery of the sources. To inform you in fact the content worthy of note we will think this valid online service. After registering for a blog, suggestions will be made automatically, even taking into account the interests that your contacts share. The merit of this opportunity lies rightly with the tags inserted in the feed. Suffice it to think that under each title there is a variety of information available, from the contents that are reported to you and that you must still read to the readers who have subscribed to the feed, without forgetting the tags, whose basic mission consists both in the suggestions blog but also in navigation between the contents.

Finally, Feedly also has the Shared Collection from her that will make you an influencer copywriter. You can tell users what you read. Consequently, they will decide whether to follow what is suggested. Such as? Via the RSS Feed button: once the address has been entered, select the key that best suits you based on the size, and indicate to the readers which updates are the most worthy of attention.

In terms of customer loyalty, what's better than this tool?

2. Keyword definition

Defining keywords and their synonyms is part of the SEO Copywriting work that should always be done upstream. There are really many useful tools in this regard. Google Ads is certainly the best known, but certainly not the only one.

- Google Ads and basic suggestions for creating a list of keywords

Known as Google Adwords until July 24, 2018, this online advertising service, created by the Colossus of Mountain View, is undoubtedly the most complete for inserting advertising spaces in the search pages. Of course, Google. The job of the SEO copywriter is to select the best list of keywords in relation to the reference advertising campaign. Doing a good job, in this sense, allows you to show Internet users, who are always potential customers, the ads most relevant to their search questions. The keywords, in this respect, must always correspond to the terms used by those browsing on Google to search for items that the customer you work for sells. Finding this keyword list on the fly is certainly not easy. For this reason, flexibility is essential for you, as you must always be ready to enter new keywords and, if necessary, change them or even remove some.

The main advice we feel we can give you is to always identify with the Internet users. Write down the core business categories of the business you are collaborating with, select the most common terms, opt for the phrases that best describe the categories is very useful to search more easily. For example, you are a copywriter who works with a company that specializes in selling sports shoes. Very well. At the classic query MEN'S SPORTS SHOES, you could add two more, like MEN'S GYMNASTICS SHOES or MEN'S RACING SHOES. After that, evaluate the trend. Are these terms used as often as Internet users access your partner's website? If the answer is negative, as we have already stated, you need to modify the list of keywords and maybe go to WINTER

SPORTS SHOES or SUMMER TENNIS SHOES. If, on the other hand, the work defined above proceeds at full speed, you can associate the previously used name with the name of the trademark of men's sneakers or men's running shoes.

To approach specific customers, the list of keywords must also be as specific as possible. Always naturally connected to the theme of the online advertisement you are about to make. Not making this job upstream is a pretty serious mistake, because you would go to lose a whole series of potential customers, perhaps even particularly profitable ones.

Still remaining anchored to the previous example, choosing as a specific word MEN'S RUNNING SHOES, you can count on an announcement that will be shown to all internet users looking for this type of sports shoes.

Also in this type of work is the interception of a specific niche that determines success.

However, as an SEO Copywriter, you should always try to reach as many users as possible, starting with specific keywords. In fact, starting with too general words does not pay, because the road to reach those who surf the internet becomes more tortuous.

The competition is getting higher and higher and you would end up squandering the budget that the company in charge puts at your disposal, given that the offer inevitably tends to rise. Experimentation, in this case, as already pointed out, is the characteristic that must never be lacking in this work.

To find the best keyword list, you need to test the results in the field.

It is good, however, to avoid the use of duplicate keywords within your account in any way possible.

Why? Well, Google shows you a single ad per advertiser, referring to a specific keyword.

Choosing SHOES as a keyword is too general, although maybe you could reach a user looking for a pair of shoes. The problem is that you would end up paying a lot for an announcement and not to conclude anything, if the person concerned doesn't make any transaction. Better to opt for example on FASHION GYMNASTIC SHOES.

Excellent strategy is that of grouping similar keywords within ad groups. When you work with Google Ads, give online surfers the chance to display more relevant ads in relation to the items of interest, it's a goal you never have to move away from: for example, create two groups of advertisements, such as DA GINNASTICA DA MAN and MEN'S EVENING SHOES. To this second group, add variables, such as ELEGANT MEN'S SHOES, CLASSIC MEN'S SHOES, MEN'S LEATHER SHOES.

This division will ensure that men's evening shoes are displayed by Internet users only when they type the last three queries and not in the case of MEN'S GYMNASTICS SHOES.

What to say finally about the number of keywords? Is there a right number of keywords for a single group of advertisements? It is not a fixed rule, but the ideal number is between a minimum of 5 and a maximum of 20.

It is preferable that each individual ad group contains the keywords directly related to the underlying theme of the group.

The variants, as singular and plural (editor's note not the case of shoes, but maybe of jacket / jackets, coat / coats) will be included automatically and there is no need to add them.

The same applies to any spelling or typing errors that can occur when the user conducts his search query.

- Ubersuggest: an essential tool to improve your blogging and SEO Copywriting activity

In the toolbox of essential SEO tools in the world of online copywriters, one of the most interesting tools in the Keyword Planner landscape is Ubersuggest (https://neilpatel.com/ubersuggest/). What is it? Of an SEO tool, developed by Neil Patel, with the aim of guaranteeing the advantageous opportunity to search for the most relevant keywords, as an expert in the field of search engine optimization.

If you are also a blogger, Ubersuggest also offers you the most interesting topics for your projects. Its operation is very simple, since it organizes as a list all the suggestions that Google has indicated in the field of queries typed by users:

At the base of everything, whether you are a particularly active copywriter in the production of commercial content or a successful blogger, there is the drafting of quality contents that intercept the needs of those who surf the web. Answer the question But what are people looking for? it is the first determining factor to obtain or to obtain good results. And Ubersuggest sets itself precisely in this context: directly from the homepage, all you have to do is fill in the three aforementioned fields: keyword, source and language. To refine the results, it is a wise choice to include in the sources what you really care about, namely shopping or the web for purely commercial or Youtube aspects, news and images for issues related instead to issues from non-profit bloggers. Below, you will always see the result with a summary of the data relating to a given keyword taken into consideration.

What makes Ubersuggest truly unique, however, is that it provides you with a wealth of useful information, from search volumes to keyword competition, without forgetting the cost per click. The reference section also allows you to view the results of Google Suggest and Keyword Planner which, if deemed appropriate, you can also filter. Two other filters are also excellent on the keywords you need and on the negative ones to remove.

At a strategic level, Ubersuggest plays a role of primary importance in SEO Copywriting, as it allows you to find the most useful keywords for your purposes, to improve Google meta tags and to present optimized content, especially on corporate blogs.

Much of the work with this tool is oriented to an analytical study of the queries made by users on the main search engines: in this way, it is much easier to identify the target with the personas. How to achieve this goal? Query Ubersuggest, depending on the topic for which you are of particular interest. Carefully examine the results and, in order to be more precise, do not take into consideration the results of the Keyword Suggest, as it is sometimes excessively dispersive as a channel. Within this list of results, what you need to carefully evaluate are the questions, shared needs and needs associated with various lifestyles. You should, in fact, start to take advantage of the selection within the boxes of each single keyword, in order to have only the bare essentials at hand. This material will obviously have to be seriously considered in your editorial plan.

But Ubersuggest does much more, since it allows you to learn about new titles, useful for your writing job: you can dissect a topic at 360 degrees, perhaps starting from general encyclopedic content and then continuing with the pillar articles, definitely more specific, and with longtail articles, connected to a specific deepening.

As for the writing of the post that you will re-elaborate from other sources, based on the suggested keywords, the use of H2 is essential to intercept the needs of the target you intend to approach, so that your attention is captured as quickly as possible. Even the search for secondary keywords and keywords related to the central topic is indispensable and Ubersuggest, never as in this case, turns out to be a valuable ally. Ditto for the more complex branches, where the presence of H3 and H4 is a sine qua non condition for the presentation of a highly structured content. If you also need a resource to present a summary or a conceptual map to accompany the text, especially in the case of longer sales-oriented articles, a resource like Coggle (https://coggle.it/) is really the non plus ultra, due to the ease with which it allows you to represent complex ideas, even via Flow Charts.

Finally, if you want to learn more about how to find secondary keywords, which variants match the main keyword, how to expand the semantic field of the central topic and how to improve the writing of content to be published online, always but not only in terms of commercial writing, well ... Ubersuggest is just right for you.

3. Online writing

Having already clear what kind of content to structure, the cut to be given to the post (emotional / persuasive or informative / rational, formal or informal), how the content list should be structured, it is good to consider what tool can do to the case yours for what concerns online writing.

Hemingway   Editor (http://www.hemingwayapp.com/) is one of the most credible alternatives to the classic Word sheet or to the CMS platform of the website where you are going to publish your ideas. The more you put down text, the longer you will be able to view various parameters, flanked by a whole series of highlights, worthy of a reflection without a doubt. Among these, it is worth mentioning the number of words (counting), the level of legibility of the content (feedback), the length of the sentences, the complexity of the periods, the repetitiveness of the words (excellent reporting of synonyms and variants), the judgment on the use of bold, italics, insertion of hyperlinks and citations (essential in the fast reading phase on the web).

4. The control of the texts

Before publishing a text online, especially if you have consulted a considerable number of sources, it is worth carrying out an accurate check. Control is a word that indicates various monitoring operations of how much you've actually knocked out.

The reason why:

- In reference to the synonyms and opposites, as well as the use of words, anagrams, definitions and citations, Dizy (https://www.dizy.com/) is one of the most reliable services ever. A dictionary containing useful information and curiosities, which really deserves to be consulted several times during the drafting of the post. For synonyms and antonyms, also Synonyms - Antonyms of the Italian language (https://www.sinonimi-contrari.it/) is an excellent source, as there are few on the web.

- As regards the repetitiveness of the words used in the text you wrote, an excellent online service is certainly Ripetition Detector 2 (http://www.repetition-detector.com/), whose primary purpose revolves around the Highlighting of excessively used words. In terms of SEO Copywriting, given the reporting of synonyms, its use is essential to avoid repetitiveness and give more verve to the reader.

- As part of Coypscape, Plagium (https://www.plagium.com/) is one of the easiest web based services to use. Clean in design and spartan in the interface this valid plagiarism detection tool gives you the opportunity to check if other authors have used the same words to explain to readers or to promote products in the form of reviews. Copy and paste the text (up to 5,000 characters, but you can also make more queries) in the appropriate internal search engine and click on Quick Search or

Deep Search, depending on whether you prefer a quick or deeper scan. If some source is too equal to what you wrote, Plagium will show you the text too similar and the percentage of words already used. Then it's up to you to replace them and rework the sentences.

5. The re-reading of the text

It has already been argued that syntax errors, as well as spelling errors, undermine the reliability of the content and seriously jeopardize the authority of the writer. In the case of a sales-oriented SEO Copywriting work, the company is the first to lose. Therefore, the re-reading of the text is essential.

Which web based tools can help you?

Free Online Spell Checker (https://www.jspell.com/public-spell-checker.html), as well as Language Tool Proofreading Service (https://www.languagetool.org/it/) are two excellent tools in the reporting of misprints Using them is right decision. Their operation is as intuitive as it is, since it is sufficient to copy and paste what you have already written and wait for the necessary time, so that these web based services give you the results.

Learn copywriting

Knowing how to write well in Italian, to respect the grammatical rules, to know the use of punctuation at best are essential requisites for becoming a successful copywriter.

But they are not enough alone.

Unlike other paths more or less related to the world of writing, from the teacher to the journalist, from the lawyer to the notary, along the same lines as for successful writers, even in the case of copywriters the path is not so linear.

This profession can develop into many branches. The basics are different for everyone.

What we want to tell you is that a degree in the humanities, an internship in an advertising agency, having already written for newspapers, owning a blog even with many visitors, a specialization course in creative or persuasive writing (we will soon deepen even better this point) as much as they help, not only are they not indispensable, but sometimes they are not decisive. Always following this logic, having just one or all the requirements listed above will not automatically make you a successful copywriter.

Useful suggestion for writing high quality content is the registration with thematic groups on Facebook or on LinkedIn. Here in fact you will be able to read a whole series of useful opinions both on sales-oriented copywriting and on creative writing, as well as on everything that revolves around the creation of an advertising campaign that has obtained the consent of the relevant public.

It is then appropriate to specialize on selected topics and it is better if these coincide with one's passions.

Moreover, it is nowadays the conquest of a niche that decrees the success on the market. And a happy and satisfied professional makes a lot more in terms of work. And commercial writing is certainly not an exception to these rules. Acting in this way, the possibility of coming into contact with companies that want to associate their brand with your writing style for the production of creative content or persuasive texts will be greater. Little but sure.

And on this aspect, having a blog can be very useful, as companies can contact you more easily.

The important thing is to produce creative, stylish, unique content on the Web, but in a constant manner.

Writing one-time or so for ... well it won't give you any noteworthy results.

Returning to the talk about the courses to follow, there are plenty of them and many of them are also online. Follow them is an extra opportunity that, especially if you are at the beginning in this sector, will allow you to stand out from the competition, because you will be able to learn the secrets of the best experts in the sector. The difference, however, is made by the desire to learn, the style of writing, having creative skills and being able to adapt, given that customer requests will always be the most varied and propose the tone of voice for the target of reference is not always easy.

Who is the skilled copywriter?

A versatile thinker who knows the language in depth, knowing how to express it with mastery over a specific channel, be it the paper, the web or other media. Just like a seasoned seducer, the writer must influence, fascinate and conquer each individual with a text.

At the same time, this communication expert can be considered as a real architect of the text, an artist of words or even a curious creative who for the whole day has to do with texts, titles, slogans, naming , headline, word games and that perhaps constantly strives to transform into words the strategies of a company or the concept of a specific brand.

Regardless of the type of product, its basic mission always remains to make users call for action.

But let's proceed with order.

In modern marketing, sales-oriented writing is essential for a company that decides to market products.

More and more companies are entrusting the copywriter with the task of writing reviews and texts to adapt nowadays mainly to the web, but also slogans for TV and radio, as well as texts for billboards and for press announcements. For copywriting jobs, entrepreneurs mostly prefer to work with advertising agencies. In fact, the copywriter increasingly works in the agency. Only a few companies prefer to have this figure within the staff.

Moreover, more and more copywriters work as freelancers. In Italy, however, less than in many European countries.

The successful copywriter is one who has creative talent, who knows how to experiment and who always has straight antennas ... Doing more than a successful job that favors the increase in sales in a company, unlike in the past, may not even be enough .

The reason? The market is constantly changing and a certain modus operandi, specific techniques for producing sales-oriented texts do not necessarily mean that they last outside.

Even in the field of commercial writing, reiterating the same model to infinity does not work.

Dropping the antennas means always considering alternative ways to effectively communicate to customers, whether actual or potential, the value of the products promoted. All even when the sales trend is positive. Knowing how to experiment is one of the many factors of success in commercial writing, because it allows you to sell in an alternative way.

The work of the copywriter

Both large companies and small and medium-sized companies, as well as start-ups, are looking for specialized figures in the field of copywriting, especially in the SEO branch.

Putting high quality content online is the easiest way to be appreciated in the eyes of customers who deserve to read well-structured texts. More and more often, in this regard, you may have read the maximum Content is King.

The real motivation is that in the era of social networks, where interactions are social in nature, sharing high-quality content is an important advantage for a company, since there are not only money at stake, but also market share, competitive advantage and brand popularity.

To achieve success in the eyes of staff recruiters, the creative qualities, the style of writing with a high persuasive and emotional impact, the experiences gained on the right and on the left are an added value.

But also the transversal competences, that is to say to be able to range in the SEO branch, in the field of visual communication or in advertising, where it is necessary to highlight the product's strengths, nevertheless represent a point in your favor, in the moment in you wish to apply for this job.

In recent times, the selection of copywriters has definitely increased, because companies aim to communicate the right content as precisely as possible. Also because then it is the company brand that benefits.

The latter, when it can count on well-written content, has the opportunity to create contact with potential customers. What we therefore want to tell you that in Italy, despite the crisis, there is certainly no lack of offers in the copywriting sector. And the same argument is also valid at world level. Therefore, if you have a perfect knowledge of English or any other foreign language and writing is one of your many passions, all you have to do is enhance your creative talent, putting yourself to the test in this area.

In terms of job opportunities, regardless of the type of communication in which he works, if he works in an advertising agency, the figure of the copywriter is almost always internalized.

It is normal for an agency worthy of the name to have a series of projects every month.

And the good copywriter will have to follow various projects.

It is therefore a work that goes well beyond the canonical 8 hours. Advertising agencies and consulting companies, in fact, do not know timetables. Try searching through job listings. In Italy and especially in Milan, the figure of the copywriter is increasingly sought after.

In an advertising agency, if the working collaboration concerns companies of a certain thickness, given the institutional cut and the formal communication, the monthly salary of a copywriter can exceed 2,000 euros. Then clearly, the pay varies from the projects you follow.

But there is not only the advertising agency among the job opportunities of the aforementioned professional figure. Even if it is an alternative to the web agency or the classic media agency, there are several companies that prefer to have a copywriter on their staff. The problem, however, is that generally this professional does everything in the branch of marketing and communication. It does not deal only with sales-oriented writing, aimed at enhancing the company's products or corporate brand, but also takes care of communication on social networks, writes tests on the company blog, defines the communication strategy on off-line channels , deals with customer assistance, draws up the marketing operational plan in collaboration and much more. On this point, in this regard, many companies should have clearer ideas.

However, more and more copywriters decide to start their own business working as a freelance.

As freelancers, they in fact have a VAT number, a very welcome requirement for companies. The main reason is that copywriting is a work that revolves around specific projects and not a continuous collaboration, day by day. Unless, as we have already had to highlight, that of the copywriter is not a figure internalized by companies and web agencies.

So, if on the one hand there are entrepreneurial realities who prefer to work on projects, giving the copywriter, as an external collaborator, the possibility of achieving a specific goal, on the other hand there is to say that there are media agencies or companies that , having understood the potential of digital well in advance, they prefer to have in the staff a figure totally dedicated to the care of communication at 360 degrees.

In any case, as a matter of flexibility, in the current state of affairs, many prefer the freelance solution, given that the work is organized and managed independently. If you are a freelancer in the field of commercial writing, you will certainly know that time and money. So, the clearer the directives, the less you will need to interface with the company on duty, since you have a perfect overview of the projects to follow, the more you will earn at the economic level. Time is money, never like in this field.

Conclusions

At this point you will certainly have a clearer overview on the field of copywriting. In reference to how to start, as we have already anticipated, a training course, fundamental for learning the basics in the various branches of this discipline, can be the turning point for you.

Listening to the experience of authoritative experts on the subject is the first step to create your own toolbox and to know where to act and how to intervene. The reading of concrete case studies and the experimentation in writing sales-oriented texts with an emotional slant is for many the launch pad in this new sector.

Are you ready to accept this exciting challenge?

Copy for business

Copywriting to sell

Writing to sell, in the era of e-commerce and social networks, has become a job in every respect.

Do you have any idea how many companies have put really excellent products on the market, often revolutionary, but which, unfortunately, are not successful, because the message conveyed does not have the desired effect, influencing the target audience?

Like it or not, companies that are unable to communicate what they produce almost never succeed in sales.

In a nutshell, entrepreneurial and managerial talent is essential to market high value and exquisite workmanship products, but without copywriting, sales feedback will not be up to par.

In order to avoid that the product you are going to put on the market does not obtain the desired success, as an entrepreneur you cannot do without commercial copy, able to best present to the customer what you are selling.

What is the job of a good copywriter?

Highlight the strengths of the product and bring out its distinctive features.

Those that, for instance, ensure your company competitive advantage. On the basis of a strategy agreed upstream between the company and the copywriter, the message conveyed may be informative, professional, descriptive or, as it happens more and more often, a more emotional one. At the decision-making level, the type of product put on the market will have an influence that is certainly not trivial.

If your company, with the support of a well-planned and efficient copywriting strategy, is able to better communicate commercial messages, it will have the opportunity to be able to increase, and even drastically, sales. All regardless of the channel used for the dissemination of promotional messages, whether off-line or online. Good writing always gives the core business of your business a little something extra.

Being able to have in your staff copywriters able to make the best use of the rules of good sales-oriented writing, makes your company make a remarkable leap in quality.

How to write to sell?

Returning to the question that is the subject of this paragraph, here are some useful tips to fully achieve your goals, as an entrepreneur.

Who should you contact?

To ensure a turnaround in your business and to boost your sales, the choice of a commercial copywriter is a decisive factor. Which business writer do you have to choose to promote the products you sell? The evaluation process that leads you to the final decision should not be absolutely underestimated.

There are many entrepreneurs who prefer to save on the budget, because they mistakenly think that all business writers are able to write. This is a wrong choice, because only a few know how to have a sales-oriented writing cut. The recruitment of a professional with proven experience, who has already reviewed products in the same sector in which your company moves and which has brought serious results to those who have requested its services, is fundamental to increase your turnover and your popularity. company, as well as to bring the product to a leading role in the market.

The creation of an advertising type message (advertising note, to be understood as making the product values public) is the primary purpose of copywriting directed to the sale. From the indefinite audience of the recipients of the message there is the target audience, composed of potential customers. Those that potentially have an interest in the product. The writing of the skilled copywriter must be targeted to this slice of audience. To achieve the goal, the good copywriter must start putting himself in the shoes of the product target,

159

foreseeing what his actual needs are. How does the relevant public act? What needs do customers have to buy this product? What are consumer habits? How do decisions are made during the purchase phase? What is the spring that then opens the wallet? Only by reasoning with the head of the target (and this is not easy), the writer will allow your company to intercept the concrete needs of the demand.

Maximizing the value-by-word

A direct style helps and not a little in the field of sales. And this is even more true for the writer. The reason? Those who read the messages often do not have much time. Moreover, in an era where you are constantly bombarded with promotional messages, the copywriting text must be distinctive. The readers and the target will not give infinite credit to your business. Indeed, it is exactly the opposite. The credit your company must take care of. And even in the shortest possible time. Based on the above, an excellent copywriting work revolves around resorting to the minimum of words, so that the greatest possible amount of information is conveyed in the message conveyed to the target audience. All of course of quality, in order to best describe the specifications of the product put on the market. Going straight to the heart of the matter, using a direct style, in fact, also rewards in terms of sales.

Bring value to your target

A winning copywriter is one who knows how to create value for the target, affecting the selective attention of potential customers. How to fascinate customers, capturing their interest? Valuing product benefits, explaining why it is necessary to have one, or guiding those directly involved in solving a problem step by step are two of the main keys to the success of an effective message. In the commercial field, transmitting value to customers allows your company to have important economic returns thanks to the written word.

Reliability?

When you rely on a copywriter to advertise your product, you must be informed in detail about his writing style. The first question you have to ask is whether it is reliable. Even in sales-oriented copywriting, reliability and authority are two fundamental parameters.

This means: impeccable Italian, absence of grammatical errors, absolute respect of the guidelines. Citing numerical and factual data in an informative post, perhaps in the sector in which your company operates, and then specifying the reason why it is worth buying what you sell, is most often a successful strategy.

For example, did a travel agency hire you to promote a last-minute package? As a good copywriter, you need to be able to write down a highly emotional post that makes readers want to visit that particular tourist destination, solving all the problems associated with a vacation, such as stress in preparing and managing the available budget.

Knowing how to write to see means being able to intercept the target your company is targeting.

And, especially on the internet (e-mail marketing, review, landing page), but also in the press and in commercial letters, a high-impact title intrigues the reader, capturing their attention. Getting the title wrong is an inadmissible mistake for a copywriter, since not attracting the interest of the reader is synonymous with loss of money for the company. Investing in the title is one of the challenges that the seller copywriter must succeed in winning.

However, clickbait should be avoided to the fullest. What is it? For many it is the worst of the web, that is to say sensationalist titles whose primary objective is to bring a large number of visitors to the website to dramatically increase the number of visits or, in the case of paid to write websites, clicks on banners .

Often phrases are intentionally adopted which suggest a totally different meaning from the content of the article. In the era of social networks, these click-capture baits are increasingly common.

And at least once, let's face it, everyone took the bait. Using this copywriting technique is a sensational own goal, because the reader, after rolling his eyes and becoming so curious to read the content, is disappointed. Beaker marketing focused on the rule that a higher number of clicks corresponds to high earnings. Leveraging on the emotional aspect of the reader, first of all anger and sadness, often completely false contents are spread in the Net universe: fakes or better buffaloes on the internet.

Product Features

A creative writing that respects itself must highlight, almost in a hammering way, what are the real benefits of the product you are marketing.

This means that the product's strengths should not be presented as a shopping list. This would bore the reader and would be counterproductive in commercial terms. Potential customers almost have to touch the distinctive features of the product. And the words of the copywriter prove to be decisive. As an entrepreneur, not considering this means wasting time and wasting money.

Emotive Communication

Excessively verbose, cold, plastered, flat, inexpressive or pumped writing styles represent the death of business. The reader gets bored and in terms of the image of your company he loses.

Writing to sell is the exact opposite, because it means involving the reader and making them dream, stimulating their emotions. In practice, explain to the reader that the product that your company has put on the market is the top. You can intercept buyer people only if you know how to involve them. And this is feasible if they are at the center of your copywriting project. Creating a narrative capable of awakening a known need in the target, but interpreted in a new light is certainly a successful strategy.

How to implement it? By providing the essential information, the real benefits of the product immediately, but only some of the details. The secret lies in not being complete: buyers are keen to discover the rest of the article independently.

Knowing how to leave shaded areas is also an art.

Many of the readers intend to understand how to reach the conclusion and, despite your persuasive style, you go to accompany them in the shadow, the latter prefer to discover independently what is the path that leads them to the real benefit. What they need.

On social networks, then, the word artist must know how to create engagement, touch the emotional side of the members of the company page.

The crucial role of storytelling

The art of being able to tell stories, able to perfectly communicate what your company values are, is very important to attract new customers. Words are decisive, but also the spectacular nature of a video shot and the power of images (if you say that a picture is worth a thousand words, there is more than a concrete motivation) they are excellent allies of good writing. The more the mix has a high emotional impact, the more the content is in line with the value of the product and the identity of the company, the more success and sales will be high

174

level. The final result of the narration must in any case always be original, in order to make the story unique and different from the others.

Clarity of words

The copywriter you hire to bring important numbers to sales must have a requirement that is a conditio sine qua non: use a clear writing style, yes with a specific vocabulary but perfectly able to reach their destination even at the often mentioned Voghera housewife . Business jargon is not for everyone. Ditto for the marketese. The clarity of words and texts is the simplest way to transmit messages that arrive at their destination and that, consequently, are understood by the target to which your company addresses. The important thing, however, is that the words you use perhaps for the presentation of a product, shine within the text, capturing the attention of the end-user.

Watch the numbers!

The skilled copywriter, especially in informative or descriptive texts, in commercial communications cannot fail to mention numbers.

Oh yes, because the numerical data are always counted.

Insert in an article the number of customers who have purchased the product, the high percentage of consumers who are reputed to be very satisfied or simply satisfied with the article they have won ... just what your company has put on the market, so to speak , it is extremely important.

Why? The numbers are always proof of the facts, they increase the level of conviction of those potential customers who are still a little undecided whether to make the purchase or to turn to the competition.

Moreover, the numbers make the work of copywriting even more concrete and testify to the previous reputation of your business reality. In short, numbers increase in order to increase sales.

A personal and identifying writing style

When a successful business copywriter writes a review, a post, a slogan, the contents of a website's homepage or landing page must always be original in content, almost creating, it must be said, a personal style in terms of communication. As an entrepreneur, he also considers this aspect, when you work with a sales-oriented writing professional. If readers immediately identify the authoritativeness of the writer, your product can only benefit from it in terms of sales results. In the advertising field, for example, word games, like those rhymes and those unexpected assonances, have always been the history of advertising. And they will always continue to do so, because they like them, they leave a smile on the lips of the reader or of those who listen to that slogan. Finally, they create buzz around the content, capturing the attention of the target.

Collection of testimonials

A sales-oriented writing style cannot do without testimonials. They must be easily identified by the reader: this means that name, surname, years, profession, city are data that must be present. Better if you also use a photo of them. After that, those who have tested the product put on the market must feel free to describe their user experience. The use of the first person with a lot of quotation marks proves to be a decisive lever to attract new customers and to boost the business volume of your company. Ultimately, in the texts created to increase sales, leaving the right space for the testimonials is one of the most effective strategies there is, since to be involved are persuasive factors that make inroads among the readers. The final message must in no way appear as an imposition, but on the contrary as an advice that your best friend would give you.

The positive feedback of those who have already tested the product, especially on the Net, are fundamental. And word of mouth is confirmed as the quintessential advertising to make inroads among consumers. The latter in fact trust much more than the opinions of other buyers rather than of any other company.

Transparency is an added value

In copywriting, the truth about the product being advertised must in no way be hidden. Likewise, you never need to go overboard with a single fact. Therefore, transparency is one of the fundamental cornerstones for the writer.

No lies, given that, especially in the internet age, it takes very little to share a negative review on a product. In the eyes of the entrepreneur who hires a copywriter with the intention of giving a boost to yours, always ask yourself the question

.

But would the copywriter buy my product? If the answer is yes, then collaboration is feasible. In support of a planned marketing strategy, lies in no way find space in any type of article.

Details are important

The texts are fundamental to attract readers and, consequently, the target you approach. However, these alone are not enough. As in any work, the details are important And in the field of sales-oriented writing, the care of the graphics must be almost maniacal.

What do we mean to tell you? Simply that the chosen layout, both online and off-line, must be clean and give a significant visual impact to the contents.

There is no better graphics than another, but a graphic that has its strong point in functionality: consolidating the commercial message and making a concrete contribution to your business is what the graphics must reveal.

Summing up, the effectiveness in copywriting work is mainly measured by the number of sales and leads procured for your business. And on these results, whether you believe it or not, the graphics must be functional to your business goals.

The importance of a call to action

When the writer writes to see, the call to action in the web world is nowadays decisive. The reason? The reader is invited to take action to become an effective customer or a lead. Among the most widespread calls to action there are of course the purchase of the product, the registration for a newsletter, the filling in of the fields of a form. The call to action must therefore be emotional and engaging. Only then will the desired effect be achieved.

Prevention is better than cure

The skilled communication professional must be proactive, anticipating all (or almost all) of the questions from the reader. The writer's sales arguments must in fact be accompanied by detailed explanations aimed at anticipating any objections of the reference target of your company. In the age of the web, an objection can be considered to all intents and purposes as a real mine. Well, it is not a hyperbole to assert that those who review your product must be able to extricate themselves from this minefield, defusing all the bombs.

Result of this modus operandi? Readers will be reassured and you will benefit in terms of sales.

For example, you are presenting an online German course that has a price higher than the competition price of 20%.

Being proactive means anticipating the objection But how come there is this price increase.

As a valid architect of the text, it will be up to you to throw down the words, possibly in capital letters and in bold, on the reasons for which to spend more is convenient, because the teachers are perhaps all native speakers or because the learning method adopted is truly revolutionary. In short, because the game is worth the candle.

Be reachable

In sales-oriented writing, leads need to be able to get in touch with your business in the easiest and fastest way.

Neglecting this aspect is a blunder that a far-sighted copywriter can never do. Landing pages without a contact form are a sensational own goal, because in most cases it involves the impossibility that the demand, represented by your target, meets with the offer (your company).

At best, those who browse online and come across a landing page, where there is no contact form, will be forced to exit the landing page, type in your company name on a search engine, to go to the homepage of your website, to move to the contact page and to write to it from there. Do you have any idea how the path to an error like this has become more tortuous? Inserting the contact form would have taken just one click.

Another own goal is to insert too many fields to fill in the form. With this strategy the CTR does not rise.

Simply enter the number of essential information. For the rest there is a telephone.

Payment method and order management

In the e-commerce era, there is some information that needs to be clear right away.

Among these, the payment method and the order management (ie shipping) are among the most important. The potential customer, once he has decided to purchase the product on the website of your company, asks himself how he can pay and when he will receive the product.

Here, in a well-structured copywriting work the aforementioned information must be easily identifiable and immediately transparent.

Are there any additional costs for shipping? Should they be spun off? Is the cash on delivery not accepted as a payment method?

The thing must be clear upstream. Do you deliver to some countries? Very well.
But everything must be put on paper. What happens if the courier does not find the customer at home when the order is delivered? Your policy must be indicated immediately. And if the product arrives

defective at destination? Or if the package arrives damaged at the address indicated by the buyer? In a sales-oriented writing job, these aspects must be specified and must be clear. In the event of any problems that depend on third parties, your company can avoid having a negative image, if everything is set down in black and white. The good copywriter must be able to translate all this into written words.

Conclusions

The aforementioned measures are valid for every type of sales communication, naturally making the necessary adjustments in relation to the specific product to be presented and the sales channel used, such as a newsletter, a page of your e-commerce site, a landing page, a brochure and so on. In short, the product changes, the channel changes, but the sales rules remain roughly the same.

In your copywriting works, always write texts that can awaken the emotions of those who read you. Use simple and fresh words that allow readers to understand how to meet their needs. And if they have none, they will begin to believe they have them because of your content. It is up to the words you will use to transport the target to which the company communicates towards the concrete benefits they will enjoy when they use the product you reviewed.

The simple characteristics of the products mentioned by way of simple list are too objective, cold and lacking in emotion. The classic bulleted list that knows a lot about the shopping list keeps people away from the purchase. As a professional in the field of content writing, it's up to you to turn features into advantages that are subjective, full of warmth and have the advantage of bringing the recipients of the message closer to the purchase.

Therefore, always focus on the contents, always devising them in relation to who the buyer personas are. Communicating in a persuasive, engaging, emotional and sincere way will get you better results from time to time. You will see that the efforts made in the field will give you great satisfaction!

Mind Hacking

This is a unique book.

What we will see in this book is a very particular and transversal topic, which can be applied to sales, copywriting, marketing of any kind.

Persuasion is critical to the effectiveness of what we do, and in this book, we will see 25 Advanced persuasion techniques that will give you access to shortcuts for the customer's mind.

You can apply these techniques on different occasions, from the simple copywriting text to the drafting of a marketing plan for your company.

It is also interesting to know these strategies to be able to recognize them when they are applied to us: these are techniques known until now only by the largest companies that will give access to incredible results.

PS: We've all been there. By reading this text, you will recognize different methods that have also been applied to you, to make you believe or buy something.

There is nothing wrong with this: you have not been deceived.

These techniques work thanks to internal mechanisms of our mind, and very often we cannot block them or recognize them when they are used.

Use this in your favor: now that you have this book, you will be able to structure your work so as to apply these strategies to maximize your results.

Finally, I ask you to use these techniques for positive purposes.

Let's be honest, in the world, these manipulation strategies are often used to deceive people. Because they work, and those who know them are tempted to take the shortest way to make them bear fruit.

However, a company that sells poor quality products or services with these persuasion strategies will be able to sell a lot, but will not have satisfied customers.
It is not a sustainable long-term plan.

Create affinity

The first technique we're going to see is one of the best known.

We often see it used, but we may never have stopped to think specifically about what it is: it is the construction of a system of affinity and empathy with the customer.

What is meant by affinity? It is simply a matter of finding and highlighting similarities between us and our client. The goal is to allow the customer to identify with us. This creates a relationship of trust that allows us to take part, indirectly, in its decisions.

A very simple example of this technique is found in some telesales: the testimonials speak, before the product, of their problems and their difficulties, which will then go to resolve with the product that the advertiser wants to sell.

The purpose of these scenes is to allow target customers to identify themselves in one of the testimonials, to make them exclaim "I too have this problem!" And the direct consequence will be "I too can solve it like this."

Abdication of responsibility

What often stops people buying is the stance, the responsibility that a wrong choice can result: the difficulty in justifying to others but especially towards you any waste of money.

This is the real strength of the affinity relationship that we can create with the customer. We, or our testimonial, there We assume this responsibility instead of the customer. The customer, coming to trust us, entrusts us with the responsibility of choosing the purchase.

And we already know what to choose!

If something goes wrong, the customer can get rid of guilt. His reaction will no longer be that of a person who has made a wrong purchase, but that of a person victim of wrong advice - this is why this strategy, although so powerful, must always be combined with a very high-quality product.

This abdication of responsibility happens all the time: just think how often we don't check the prices we are offered, *trusting* that the person we deal with is proposing us, if not a low price, at least fair?

This also happens when, for example, we rely on a lawyer to safeguard our interests. How do we know, if we are not experts in the field, that he is really acting in our interest?

We do not know. But it is convenient to assume that this is the case: the alternative is to undertake the study path that led the lawyer to be who he is now; a decidedly impractical solution.

The first step is, therefore, to find affinity with the client: let us take an interest in him, and see how we can build it.

We can also use this technique in copywriting: let's start from our target to understand who are the people who will read our text, and consequently analyze what are the points on which we can leverage.

What interests the customer?

Ok, so we need to see what the points are in common between us and the customer. But not all points are important in the same way: having brown hair is certainly not an affinity that we can use to leverage on his mind.

According to Dan Kennedy, the subjects that interest people are simple, and they are always the same.

- Family
- Work
- Interests
- Money

In this order.

And this is the order we should follow to start a discussion that will lead us to create an affinity relationship.

The first thing is always the family. More for women than for men, but in general it is statistically the topic that people care about most.

Then we can take an interest in employment. What do they do in life? What role do they have in their company, and how does this shape their day?

We continue: we now move on to free time. If we identify a hobby, a sport or any common recreational interest, we can talk about this. Common interests are extremely effective, and it is relatively easy to build affinities in this way: it is sufficient to be prepared on some basic topics - such as football, in Italy, to create a relationship with the vast majority of people.

Finally, we move on to talk about money, politics, the economy. It is important that this point be the last to talk about: before making an economic request, or any kind of commitment to our interlocutor, we must have created an affinity in the family, in work, and in interests.

This will incredibly increase our chances of success.

Indirect affinity

Do we have points in common with the interlocutor?

It is not a real problem. We cannot expect to have points in common with all people, in all the necessary subjects.

One trick we can use, however, is indirect affinity.

We use points in common with other people we know! It sounds incredible, but it really works.

"Do you have a daughter? Even my sister has one, now I'm looking for a photo. "

A phrase of this type, although it cannot create a direct affinity, serves the same purpose and, incredibly, does not diminish the effectiveness of the affinity connection we are creating.

Transparency and intrigue

The purpose of this is to convey transparency: we must be transparent to our interlocutor, to allow him to trust us.

In particular, if we are a public figure, it is useful to be transparent with what are our faults or otherwise they could be perceived as such.

In fact, very often these traits are not really negative, except when we try to hide them. This works particularly well in politics: aspects of the character's private life are often communicated in a negative light if this is done by opponents.

This is obviously not possible if the politician in question has always been transparent in this regard: if everything is known, there is nothing to discover. In this case, we are sure that nothing can be used against us.

On the contrary: these aspects (we can say, improperly, *defects*) can create relationships of affinity, as we have seen previously.

People will identify with us if they are related to us in this respect. And, even if for them this is a cause for shame, it should not be for us; it is important that they know that they will not be judged differently on the basis of these aspects, because they are simply shared also by their interlocutor.

If on the one hand, transparency plays in our favor, on the other we also want to keep a veil of mystery about our person to intrigue people.

Creating an aura of mystery around our figure leads people to want to know more about us.

This keeps them "around" us, and gives us the opportunity to meet them, to talk, to communicate and to sell.

The solution is, therefore, to balance the two things, transparency, and mystery, and exploit both these aspects.

If we are 100% transparent, people will lose interest quickly and forget us. On the contrary, if we are too mysterious, people will not trust us.

Flattery and licenses

To hear the people the desire to be with us, and make them feel our lack when we are not, we must ensure that they feel better when we are with them.

Each person's hidden desire is to be - or to feel - better than others.

What we need to do is give them this permission. They must understand that we know, and that we agree, that they are better.

Not good people: people better than others, or at least most of the others.

We must, therefore, give them the license to feel in a way that they normally do not feel free to feel, to think in a way that they reasonably believe does not have the right to do.
But with us, they can, and we understand them.

This is also true in many other contexts: helping people to justify themselves in their comparisons is extremely useful.

It may seem trivial, but many people have this problem: they hear something that they rationally believe is wrong.

Or they would like to behave in a way that their mind knows is not right.

If, when they are with us, they are allowed to be like they want to be, to do what they want to do, we can be sure that they will look for our company in the future.

Everyone wants to be special

A special case of this strange permission system is the lure.

People like to be considered special.

This aspect recalls a text by Blair Warren, which lists 6 steps that are followed to request the participation of a person in a cause. This system relies on the need for these people to be considered - by others but also by themselves - special.

1 Explain the situation in its entirety and
2 make it clear what the problem you want to
solve

3 Explain the role the donor can play in this
situation

4 Emphasize the importance of this role, so
that you can understand, indirectly, that the
person is important to your cause

5 Explain why you believe the person you are
talking to is right for that role

6 Ask if you can count on him

A particular technique that can be used
is *conditional flattery.*

It's very simple: a person is complimented, but this is only valid if he agrees to do what we want.

An example is a phrase like this:
"We know we can count on you because you are a good person who cares about this issue."

Create a ritual

This is very common in ... religions!

Creating a ritual is an incredibly effective way to retain people and make them feel the need to be there, to participate.

This thing works. It has been used, perhaps purely by chance, over the centuries. Just think of the importance of parties, ceremonies, events that have been made real rituals.

We don't even realize it: we want to participate, we don't know why, but we know we want to be there.

227

This behavior has been taught to us since we were children: just think of the school; the uniforms, the strict schedules, the interval. We felt part of something.

We make people feel part of something, and they will continue to want to feel that way. It doesn't matter if it's something stupid: most religious rituals are difficult to justify rationally, but they work.

Creating a ritual guarantees that people continue to follow us, because the detachment from this ritual, which they are now used to, is something they want to avoid.

Symbolism

Linked to the importance of rituals is that of symbolism.

This is a simple concept, but it is often ignored or not applied properly.

Just think of the most valuable brand in the world: Apple.

Apple presents itself, in many ways, as much more than an electronics company.

Owning an iPhone does not mean having the ability to call, send messages, and all the new features that other manufacturers sponsor.

Owning an iPhone is a symbol, and that's enough.

Apple does not promote the features, functionalities or specifications of its phones: it is sufficient to let people know that there is a new iPhone.

Symbolism does the rest.

Demonstrations

The demonstrations are very important. We think of telesales - none of us probably want to look like teleshopping, yet these are designed and structured to sell, and they really work.

What we don't know, and that doesn't matter even if we know it, is that very often these demonstrations are distorted.

They could also represent the product in a case of real use, but for these tests, the ideal conditions were created to obtain the desired result.

Moreover, very often, especially if we have the opportunity to record these demos, we will happen to do repeated tests. And of course, the final version will be the one with the best result, not necessarily the most realistic!

We, therefore, remember: we prove that our product works. It doesn't matter if the proof is mounted ad-hoc, and it doesn't matter if we fear it can be discovered too easily.

People want to believe that what we sell really works, so they can solve their problem.

We must give them the material they need to believe it.

The numbers count

It is easy to believe that if a large number of people believe in something, this is true.
It is not logical or correct reasoning, yet it works. Very often we also do it unintentionally.

Therefore, if a large number of people have bought, or used, one of our products, this must be of good quality.

It is therefore very useful to indicate these numbers in the sale. Let's think about how many times we read phrases like "*Chosen by over one million customers.*"

This means nothing, except that the company is able to sell the product. However, sentences of this type are extremely effective and create what is called *social proof*.

What is interesting is the total absence of logic in statements of this kind.

We know that the product has been chosen by one million customers. But is a million customers a lot or a little?

The reference market could be composed of 5 million people as of 5 billion. They could have presented the product to 100 million people to convince then only 1% of the purchase.

We, therefore, understand that the number, without a context around it, is simply meaningless. Yet it is extremely effective because it *seems* *like* a high number.

Another important aspect to consider is that the number is more important than the action: if one million customers have purchased our product and, of these, 100,000 still uses it after 10 years, indicating the second digit logically has more meaning important: it suggests that these people are very convinced of the value of the product and demonstrate it, using it after a certain period of time.

However, the number is lower.

The fact is, the number counts more than the context. If we can then formulate a text with a larger number, the result will be better; it doesn't matter if the concept is less interesting.

I told you

In this chapter, we will see how to always be right and gain the trust of our customers even on forecasts for which they should not trust us.

The principle behind this logic is that on which horoscopes, astrologers and in general all these people who say they can predict the future are based.

The same is also true in more formal environments, from which we would expect a more serious and responsible behavior

(Wrong! Actually we assume that this is the case because we trust).

The principle is very simple: if I guess once, it doesn't matter how many times I did wrong.

We can make dozens of predictions on the value of shares, cryptocurrencies, on the expansion or contraction of markets, on trends and much more.

If even one of these is true, we will all be known as "the one who predicted the X boom."

It matters little if we have also foreseen another ten booms that did not actually take place.

Moreover, the same can also be done in the dimension of time. We may have been extremely successful for a short period of time. It doesn't matter, let's use that.

Were our forecasts correct and effective in March 2017? Let's take March 2017 as an example of our abilities.

We decide what to write in our sales letter, or what to talk about in our event. We, therefore, choose, without problems, the arguments that bring us the most advantage - our competitors do the same.

A particularly interesting example is that of gambling. Think of the Superenalotto: sometimes you hear of millionaire winnings, and many people are tempted.
What is not said, but that we all know well, is how much capital players spend to create these jackpots.

The number of people losing to the Superenalotto or the number of games that do not bring substantial victories is not advertised. We only talk about the positive aspect, when we all know rationally that the other side of the coin has a much greater economic weight.

The authority

Who writes, sends, says or in any way communicates the message, is extremely important.

The person or company from whom everything starts counts.

Choosing a good source for ours is fundamental. The idea is to be ourselves the source we need: in this case, the people who receive the message trust us, give value to our communications and therefore pay particular attention to what we say.

But this is not always the case.

Especially if we are starting out, we cannot expect the recipient of our message to listen to us. Because he doesn't know who we are.

In this case, we need to take the authority of someone else.

The positive note is that there are several ways to do it, and it is extremely easy.

We can hire testimonials or influencers to promote our brand. The unconscious reasoning that potential customers will do is that if a service is produced and promoted by an authoritative person, then it must be quality.

And this allows us to become authoritative ourselves in our sector.

And so far it may seem obvious. What is not considered, however, is that the medium through which communication takes place also counts.

Being on TV, for example, gives us very important credibility. And it is not only due to the number of people reached but also to the impression we give of ourselves.

The same happens with trade magazines: if we are published on Forbes, it doesn't matter who the journalist who wrote about us is. There is transferred authority from the magazine itself because this is positively evaluated by readers.

It is also interesting to note that the same transfer of authority takes place with paid advertisements: being on Forbes because a journalist wrote about us is extremely difficult, while anyone can be there by purchasing advertising space. Yet the effectiveness is the same!

We and them

A further strategy, often used in politics or in the social sphere, is that of dividing the world into two factions.

Good and bad, beautiful and ugly, honest and dishonest. It doesn't matter if the type of division makes sense or not, nor does it matter if there are more factions or even none.

Dividing people between "us and them" is a great way to create a sense of belonging.

A very effective strategy to achieve this is to create an enemy. We can identify a person, an opponent or a competitor, and exploit it to our advantage, presenting ourselves as the saviors of our customers towards this person.

It is important that this enemy is identified as a single entity. Let's say for example "we and them", not "us, group 2, group 3, etc." Similarly, we talk about "us and the competition," not about "us, the competitor 1, competitor 2" and so on.

This aspect is fundamental because we must present ourselves as able to help, to *save*, our listeners. We should not present ourselves as one of the alternatives, but as the only choice to avoid *something very bad*.

Buying resistance

We now introduce the concept of resistance threshold. What is it?

It's simple: in order for a person to move forward towards the purchase, it is necessary for her to overcome various barriers that tend to hold her in place.

For example, we opt for the following: our system for acquiring customers consists of an advertisement on Facebook that leads to a page that asks for an email, after 4 emails we try to close the sale.

The first step for the user is to click on one of our advertisements: relatively low threshold, so we can expect a good percentage of people to do it (compatible with the statistics of the medium).

The second step is to insert an email. This is private data, which some people tend not to leave easily. So the threshold is slightly higher; however, the fact that the person has clicked on the advertisement and is there to see our page is a sign of interest.

We can raise this threshold further, if we deem it appropriate, asking in addition to the email also other information such as name and surname.

After that, our lead will receive our emails. In this case, we have an advantage because by default it will not be removed from the list (there is a threshold of "annoyance" that it can bear). However, we must also make sure that you read our emails to get to the purchase.

Finally, we want you to end up buying by reading the text of our last mail.

We can see these thresholds as steps: a higher step is more difficult to climb but puts us in a position of advantage.

If on the page where we ask for the email address, we also ask for the name, we risk losing a part of our potential contacts. On the other hand, the contacts we end up receiving are the ones really interested in our product, and it's easier for them to end up buying.

We must, therefore, structure our plan so as not to place the customer in front of thresholds, insurmountable steps, but we must not even simplify the process too much and not require an investment in terms of time and attention on his part: if we do not have his own be careful and not even willing to read our emails, how do we expect you to buy?

Tip: if we use the telephone in our business, a pre-recorded message represents a much lower threshold than the interaction with a person.

Proceed by steps

But what are these steps, these steps that the potential customer must climb?

Possibilities: it is necessary to let the potential customer know that there is the possibility of doing what we propose, or that our product simply exists.

Benefit: we must now make it clear what the benefit of our product is, or the advantage that the buyer will have after having purchased it.

Reachability: we must then make it clear that it is possible to really achieve the result

- not as a bet (a lottery), but as a real possibility that we are offering to our customers

Personal possibility: ok, it can be done. But can I do it myself? Even if I'm poor? Even if I'm low? Even if I live in the countryside? We must take away all these doubts from our potential customer so that he can identify with our proposal

Difference: if the customer already has negative experiences with our competitors, we must explain why it will be different with us.

We must defeat the skepticism that created the one who came before us, and at the same time create it towards our competitors

Personal benefit: it is different from the generic benefit. We have to make our customer think about what will happen after buying our product. Not only what will he buy, but also how his life will change

Timeliness: ok, then you must buy it. Wait, you have to buy it NOW. We must provide valid reasons why taking time is not wise. In this case, we can also integrate a concept of scarcity, as we have seen.

The moral: ok it's all nice, I can do it. But will I do it? Many people are blocked, involuntarily, from what they believe to be right or wrong, lawful, and unlawful.

It is not a question of legality: obviously, we have to sell legal products and services. It is a problem of preconceptions, which we must dismantle or guide towards the direction that can allow the client to achieve his goals. Possibly passing by us.

Being aggressive?

Our first goal is to have our contact accept more information.

In fact, if we are excessively aggressive with the promotion before the potential customer has decided to learn more, we risk being too aggressive and making the customer "close."

We must, therefore, wait, and start the most aggressive sale only after the potential customer has accepted and shown a minimum of interest in knowing what we have to offer.

This is very evident in door-to-door sales, which are not widespread: the seller's first goal is not to start talking about the product and what it can do for the buyer, but it is to interest the potential buyer enough to accept learn more.

The same happens in online sales. For this reason, we use lead generation, relatively low-cost contacts that we can then educate, usually via email.

The final goal is that of selling, but we must not start from there: we make the customer

interested in the product so that it is than
he who wants to know more about it.

The false alternative

People like to be in control. Or at least believe you have it.

This strategy consists of placing the person in the situation of having a choice; the trick is that we create this situation.
You will still believe that you have chosen, but will have chosen by force, one of the alternatives that we have decided before - both must be positive options for us.

What kind of alternative can we offer our customers to make sure they have options that always play in our favor?

Here are three variables we can work on:

- Product selection, when we simply offer two different products (or a product sold in a different format, for example with a bonus)
- Choice of time, for example, the customer can choose to receive the service now or have it within three months
- Choice of benefits, when the customer may need an additional

service that may be more expensive,
but even the basic one is fine for us -
after all, pay for it!

Greedy is OK

We can choose different levers to motivate people to buy and take action.

One of the most important is greed.

People like to save or earn money, there is little to say.

And offering discounts or free products is an extremely effective method to attract potential customers and make them aware of our product.

It matters little if the discount we are offering is not credible or plausible. A discount of 70% would be excessive for most of the products in circulation if you do not *cheat* on the original price. But this is not a problem: buyers do not care if the original price is different from the day before; most buyers won't even notice.

This is what happens at Christmas time or near events like black Friday.

People care about saving so much and taking a high-value home. The fact is that we decide the starting price!

A product of € 1000 discounted by 80% has a perceived value of € 1000, while a product of € 200 that is not discounted remains a product of € 200.

As in many other examples we have seen, the rational component has very limited importance.

Part of this strategy is the provision of free services. For example, free shipping in online purchases.

Rationally, it is obvious that the cost of shipping is included in the price of the product. No salesman would be stupid enough to forget about it. Yet offering free shipping provides an incredible boost to sales.

We, therefore, take advantage of this magic word. As usual, it doesn't matter if it makes sense or not!

New is always better

In the same way as "free," even "new" is a word we can use to push people to buy.

It happened to us all: who should buy the latest fashion clothing, who should have the new iPhone model, etc.

The longer the wait, the greater the expectations for novelty, the easier it will be to complete the sale.
It doesn't matter if the new product is interesting, better or useful, there will be those who buy it just because it's new.

The purchase of a new product that we have craved for so long is a satisfaction, but this feeling starts to fade quickly, and we soon need a new product.

The ego of the customer

This technique relies on the social position of our client.

People continually confront each other, whether this makes sense or not.

This approach is widely used in companies that manage a sales force: rankings are always drawn up and prizes are awarded to the best sellers. When these are removed, the performances of all the sellers are lowered, not only those of the best.

The same also happens in the private sphere: we want to have that extra thing, the car, the pool, which our neighbors don't have. And when we have it, the same thing happens to them: in a short time the whole neighborhood ends up buying what we thought would have distinguished us.

The social status that our product can confer is very important and can lead us to many sales because our customers will like the fact that they can somehow feel superior to their friends, their colleagues, their neighbors, etc.

Furthermore, this technique goes very well with the rituals and symbolism we talked about a little while ago: just think of the ritual of an award ceremony or a cup or brooch that symbolizes our victory.

The effectiveness of these awards is that they can prove to be better than other people, and everyone can do it at least in a very specific field. The desire to be considered the best motivates and motivates people to do their best.

Sense of urgency

The fear of losing an opportunity is often stronger than the interest in the opportunity itself.
This concept may seem counterintuitive, but it is true and demonstrated.

Just think of how many occasions you play on the concept of scarcity: tickets for a concert by a famous singer will end right away, and if we're undecided we run the risk of buying them anyway because we don't have time to think about it too much.

278

The same reasoning is applied to limited edition products, which always have a greater appeal. It matters little if the limited edition is actually composed of millions of copies.

This concept is particularly strong when combined with a discount, as we saw earlier: if this discount is only valid for a limited time, it will be much easier to convince our leaders to buy. This is why Amazon, as well as much other e-commerce, always communicates when the product is about to end, and why the famous *flash offers* are so effective.

Destabilize the customer

Very often, the customer does not believe he needs our help.

During the information phase of the client, we must, therefore, instill in him also different doubts. He must come to doubt himself and his ability to successfully complete his work or achieve his goal.

And very often it really is. Let us imagine working with an entrepreneur who leads a successful company: for a person in his situation it is easy to think of being able to manage all aspects of his company, and therefore he will believe he does not need our advice.

The reality may be that his company, although well managed, could have achieved even better results with a different approach, or that the growth that makes him so sure of himself is actually slowing down, or that he is simply always positive, but less positive of the competition (therefore it is in an expanding market, and its company grows more slowly than the market, so it is actually losing shares even if the turnover increases).

The same can be done in many other ways and contexts. The key is, therefore, to make our potential customer think we need us: otherwise the decision is already made, and it is a "no."

(False) assumptions

We are literally full of beliefs, which are rooted within us. Let's take any topic: all we know about it is actually our opinion.

Ok, sometimes these opinions are formed on the basis of facts, but very often it is not so simple.

However, it doesn't matter: the important thing is to know how to recognize them and exploit them in our favor.

For example, it is much easier to sell a security system to a paranoid person than to another person who tends to feel very safe.

Whether this paranoia is justified or not does, it not matter: even if it were, it would be very difficult to make the second person change his mind - much more difficult than looking   for new customers   paranoid elsewhere.

When we try to define our client in detail, therefore, we keep in mind his beliefs, what he has spent in life and how this can provide him with the conditions for the future, the bases on which he will make future decisions.

Familiarity

In this chapter, we will see a very important concept: that of familiarity.

It is much easier for people to reason by referring to products, models, and concepts they already know.

Referring to something that is known, allows us not only to make ourselves understood more quickly but also to create a connection between us and the other party.

Instead of referring to abstract discourses, therefore, it is advisable to be practical and speak with real examples and analogies that people know.

The effort to understand something new is, for many people, excessive. And they will unintentionally stop listening to us, making all our communication useless if they understand that what we are saying is different from what they are used to. Moreover, they live well even this way.

The idea is yours

You have to find ways to get the customer to think about what you want. But he doesn't have to notice it, it must seem a natural process.

There are different ways to do this, and they all work on the lack of logic in some arguments.

People are used to making connections that are often unmotivated, yet they seem rational.

For example, we tend to believe that a well-dressed person in a suit and tie has more power. In reality, it is not necessarily so.

Yet, in sales, it is shown that this type of clothing really produces better results.

The same can apply to any type of assumption that people tend to do in an automatic way: let's think about it, let's try to find a logical connection between the starting point and the point of arrival.

If it is not there, we have found an element that we can use in our favor to make people understand something we don't really say - and that can be true or not.

The magic word

There is a magic word that gives credibility and reinforces any statement.
This word is "why." ·

Several scientific tests have been made in this regard, such as the famous experiment of the printer queue: in an office, 94% of people are willing to give us a precedence in the queue at the photocopier, if in the sentence to ask them we say "why." Otherwise, this percentage drops to 60%.

The interesting thing, though, is not this.

It turns out, in fact, that what is said after the "why" does not matter.

The same test was repeated with these sentences:

- "Because I'm late for a meeting"
- "Because I have to make photocopies"

The second sentence is practically useless. It does not add information, not a reason for the urgency and why this person should pass us by.

Guess what is the success rate of the second sentence?

94%, exactly like the first one.

The word "why" is simply magical. Let's use it as much as possible, even when what comes next is meaningless.
It is "why" that matters, not why.

Hopes and fears

This technique is extremely powerful and can be applied to both physical products and services, both in B2B and in B2C.

People tend to believe what they hope for. And they hope not to make what they fear to happen.

The desire to make a purchase is as strong as it is important for the person, the thing that he risks losing if he does not proceed with the purchase.

A simple example is the burglar alarm: we don't really care that it sounds when someone enters the house. Or rather, he has to do it, but that's not why we buy it.

We buy it because we want to avoid losing our possessions, so for the hope of defeating our fear.

Time investment

There is direct proportionality between the time we spend with our lead and its probability of finalizing the purchase.

And the more time they spend with us, the more they will be satisfied after buying.

This obviously applies to live, but also to online sales. We record videos or write long articles: if we keep them interesting, the potential customer will have invested a great deal of time in us. After spending hours, days or months reading our articles, watching our videos, they will have no choice but to buy.

Otherwise, they would have lost all this time!

This aspect is also extremely valid for increasing the price of our product, so it is important to be extremely careful with the content we disseminate.

Email Marketing

A Great Opportunity

Before talking about email marketing, we need to understand why it is better to focus on this tool and not using social media, for example.

The email or 'electronic-mail' was created with the intention of facilitating a conversation while maintaining an 'intimate' style. This is an imitation of when paper letters were exchanged through the mail or passed by hand. It gives a feeling of trust, security and confidence between the sender and the recipient.

299

It's also a much more professional tool than a social platform, since its sole purpose is to put two people in conversation through an online 'letter' system. The email is a tool with a great potential that we can still exploit. However, it is very important to understand when and how to use it; The possibility that our email will be opened in the first hour of being received is very high, while as time passes the chances of someone opening and taking an interest in our proposal falls dramatically.

Therefore, creating email marketing means creating campaigns and marketing strategies using email, without spam, as a main tool. Through this tool, we can take advantage of various methods to send our customers a clear and direct message. The most common method is the newsletter, which we will discuss later. Email marketing is considered to be the best method to retain customers. It has a very high percentage of return on investment (ROI) compared to other techniques because it is an easy, fast and direct tool when used to promote an offer, proposal, novelty, price list, etc. Furthermore, it also allows us to visualize how many people are interested in our offer when we see who has opened the email. We can practically monitor our strategy in real time.

When described, it seems like a medium for everyone and it is!

However, there are several errors that many people make, which consequently has a negative impact on the ROI. One of these common errors is email spam. Just think: a person has voluntarily registered and is interested in our proposal, but after a few days they have 20 emails from us with all the various offers ... It is very intrusive, and we are going to suffocate what should be our success. It is better to send even a single email that better describes who we are, what we do and what we offer.

What is a Newsletter

The newsletter is a very widespread tool in the marketing sector. Its main objective is to keep our customers updated. We can present new offers, products and promotions, among other things, to customers who have explicitly asked to stay updated on our business. This avoids excessive spam of intrusive and useless messages. The newsletter can be used not only to present news, but also to provide information, such as assistance for a product.

Therefore, it is a very advantageous tool for companies that want to keep their customers up to date on specific products or promotions, but it is also an advantage for professionals who are looking for advertising and new customers. Creating your own newsletter campaign does not require a high level of investment, since it is an inexpensive tool, but it requires a commitment to creating an email that attracts customers. To take full advantage of the newsletter it is best to write a short message with easy words that can be read within a short time. It should be easy to read for any type of customer and above all it invites people to take a better interest in our proposal, so that they can become potential customers in the future. At the beginning of this email we must say what we are proposing in an intriguing way. We must express the details of our event and what products or offers we want to propose. Of course, it is essential to use newsletters, but this does not mean we should underestimate all other means of email communication we can use to present ourselves to the market in the best possible way.

Have you ever thought of how many newsletters arrive to you every day? I'll give you a small example of someone accepting the conditions for us to send emails to them 'without them knowing'. They are looking for a free online ebook with the main topic "production". They come across a site where you can download the book at no cost. They click the download button ... But the file was not downloaded because they did not register with the site. So, there is a pop-up button to register. To register and download the book, they must provide an email and a password to to log in every time. They have provided their email, and over time they will find several emails from the free ebook download site. The sites or other sources we register with to obtain a product is where most of our emails come from.

Set Goals

The first thing that needs to be done before starting any economic activity is setting a clear, fixed goal. We must know what we want to gain, why we are doing this and if it is really worth investing time and money or if it is simply a waste of time. Then we may put in place all the plans we have thought of through the various resources available and the various investments. Since email marketing is a very complex tool, before realizing our plans we should understand how we want to use this system and what we want to achieve. For example, we have adopted a system to:

- Increase the number of customers who see what we want to offer every day
- Promote your brand through promotions and offers
- Make ourselves known to new people
- Increase sales

We must therefore set ourselves some goals of where we want to arrive, but with our feet on the ground, avoiding useless objectives to which we will never arrive. For objectives such as those I listed above we should try to establish a time frame in which we want to complete all these goals. This is so we can properly organize the structure of the activity, monitor the progress of our journey towards what we are aiming for and understand why we are doing what we are doing.

The goal of an activity is not always profit oriented, such as in associations, which may have a purpose in helping the community. However, in our case the main objective is to achieve a profit, we are profit oriented. This is making money through the sale of products or services. However, we are not always able to reach our goals. This can happen when the various costs are too high and are greater than revenues. What can be done in this case is to start over with a new, well-structured marketing plan and learn from the mistakes made in the past.

Transactional Emails

Transactional emails are emails that inform us of a determined action that we have accomplished or of what is missing for the compilation of a fact. Compared to commercial emails, this type has a higher open rate, since they are not intended to promote something new but simply to inform about a fact already chosen by the customer. The transactional emails are, for example, emails that notify us and confirm when we have changed the password of our account, when we have correctly registered to a site or when we have successfully placed an order and it has been sent. This type of email contains useful information for the customer and has the task of reminding the recipient that he is our client, updating him on the various facts and promotions we are proposing. We can insert a small timed promotion in this type of email, for example: "You have registered on our site! To thank you we have prepared for you a 30% discount voucher on the next purchase you make from us, valid until next week!" so as not to lose it.

Or they can simply be confirmation emails, for example when we register for an online service and are asked to verify the email address we entered by clicking the link in the email sent. In the first few lines of the email we need to describe the contents of the latter.

What is the Online Form

When a customer registers on our site, we can choose certain information that he must provide us in order to use our service. We can ask him for his email, his name and surname, his age, where he lives and what work he does. We then present him with a form to complete with all his personal information, this is an online form. This information can be very useful for getting to know the customer we are addressing and understanding what type of offer we can propose and when, so that our proposal be successful. For example: Maria is 35 years old and works in a shop where she is a hairdresser. To understand what kind of offer to make them first we need to know the age and profession, in this case 35 years and hairdresser. The question is ... what kind of product could we propose?

We could offer a product that could be useful for her work or for leisure time, such as an innovative latest-technology hair dryer at a price not too high, perhaps adding a promotion. We certainly have a much better chance of encouraging Maria to buy from us if we offer her something that can actually be useful for her work or leisure, instead of presenting her with a useless object that can serve no purpose, for example, a product that can be used by another person. Therefore, it is essential to ask questions to your client to understand what kind of product might be of interest to them and actually be useful to them.

The Autoresponder

When we talk about Autoresponders (automatic answer), we mean all messages (emails) that are sent in response automatically using an external software. This type of message serves to answer questions, needs and requests that are often made to us and to avoid handwriting the same thing to all the questions we are asked. We can set up a software that is tasked to automatically send a reply email with the message chosen by us for every need and every time a customer has a common question to ask us. Maybe in a day we find ourselves with 20 emails that have practically the same content, that have

319

asked us the same question. Why answer each email individually and waste time when we can safely set a bot to do it, so that we can think about other problems and above all how to promote our business and find new customers. An example of an Autoresponder is when we register at a website and we must confirm our email via the electronic mailbox, or simply the welcome message that is sent to each individual user who has registered to a particular service. Think about having to welcome and explain your activity to every single person who registers in our service, it would be a mess. Autoresponder messages are chosen by us and used automatically. An example could be: "Welcome to our consulting service, we hope to be of help in all cases! If you need assistance, you can contact us at the email address below." or "The request for the creation of the account on our site has been sent ... Immediately confirm your email by clicking the button below". (etc.)

These messages can also be surveys or customer questions, to keep them the same each time. The only thing you should do is to change the name of the recipient each time.

Spam: How to Ruin Yourself

Spam is sending one or more messages, usually for advertising purposes, repeatedly on e-mail. From customers it is very annoying because it is very intrusive. Almost every day on our e-mail we receive at least two spam messages (advertising), which clogs the email inbox. Some of these emails are also unsafe, in fact many have a main objective to obtain information and steal personal data from people. Obviously when we talk about spam, we are not referring only to spam via email but also to on social networks and others. We can therefore establish that spam has, as its main objective, to reach many users and try to attract them to buy. But how do they find us? Simple, we are the ones who open the doors to these people. When? Just think of all the times we have left our email address in various sites to have a service offered by the site only by registration, or when we leave our phone number to win a contest. This is why it is important to take a look at the terms of certain sites. When we register to use a service they write "the email address provided, may be subject to a transfer to a third party". It's clear where all those emails or advertising calls come from. One way to avoid being subject to these advertisements is a temporary email that we can provide to the sites so that the advertisements are not addressed to our email, but to another email that will be self-destructed after a period of time that we use. This service can easily be found on certain sites that offer this benefit. Another useful function that is directly processed by the Gmail team is the anti-spam filter, which automatically deactivates and eliminates all those annoying advertising emails that we have not chosen to be sent to us. Spam aims to send a message to many unknown people who are certainly not in the least interested in the service or product. In chapter 2 we will understand better why it is important to aim for a suitable target and why sending your own promotional message to more people is to be avoided. In summary, to avoid ruining your online reputation and looking like a person who needs money and who doesn't know where and how to advertise their services or products, it's best to avoid unnecessary spamming to random and totally unknown people.

Customer Trust

Have you ever wondered if you really know your customers? Have you ever wondered if you're talking to the right people? If your visitors are really interested in your product or service? Some time ago it was very common to take a large number of unknown emails without exact origin and send them all a promotional message: practically a senseless choice and useless spam. (It would be better to send no more than 2 promotional emails per week). While we were the first to find our customers through spam, advertising and word of mouth, today it is no longer the case. In fact, it is the consumer who chooses from who to contact and who to buy for their needs. The advertisement issued by the seller serves only to give an idea, to promote a product that lists the utilities and the advantages and serves above all to show the public that we are better than the competition.

But this can only mentally influence the client's situation, in fact it is he who decides who to choose and through advertisements they get a better idea of what we offer. So, our success is determined above all by how we address customers, the reputation we have built over time and feedback from various buyers. Therefore, customers gain for themselves through the trusting relationship they have with us. To build a good reputation with customers, we must always be sincere and available on everything, such as being clear and sincere about all the purchase prices that are present before making any purchase.

Call to Action

The 'calls to action' are the action calls, that is all the buttons and links that have the purpose of calling the potential customer to one action, and then to complete a series of actions that we want. Such as those buttons where it says: "read on", "contact us" or "buy now".

Now I will list a series of tips to best set up your call to action and attract more people accordingly.

• Choose an appropriate contrast between the colors that differs from the rest of the site, or any other means of transmission. Setting colors that don't bother the eye and that are pleasant to look at is very important; in particular, avoid making two light colors close together since it reduces readability and increases visual discomfort.

• Try different types of call to action to understand which are liked by the customers, because if you like it, that doesn't mean visitors will like it too.

• Create a simple, direct and easy to identify call to action that attracts attention in a pleasant way

• Use a clear and pleasant font

• Make your call to action an unrepeatable opportunity, a timed offer that invites the potential customer to click on it.

- Write the advantages of registering for the advertising campaign, such as: 'Register now and get 1-month free trial.'

It is important to choose a design that unites the call to action and the site or platform in general. For example: The predominant color of your software is green, and the platform is white. Your button could be green with the white sign written in the center of it to match the platform.

Our Strengths: SWOT Analysis

Not everyone always manages to achieve their goals, since marketing strategies are not always adequate for their business. For this reason, even if we have great potential and talent, we cannot exploit it because we do not have the means or customers to achieve our goals. To understand why this is happening, we need to do a self-analysis, which means we must look at ourselves with the eyes of visitors and customers. It seems to us that everything is fine, that our products or services are actually useful to the customer, or that the way and the means by which we address the customer is perfect. However, in reality it is not, and this is confirmed to us by the number of sales and earnings registered each month.

The SWOT analysis determines the abilities, strengths and weaknesses of our economic activity and we have competition, and therefore also the strengths of those around us. The strengths of an activity or a small business are special features that make a positive difference from the competition; therefore, they are advantages that we can use against the competition. They can be for example:

• Certain skills or talents we possess to make a product or service in a better way than others

- A good reputation at the product or brand level

- If we have made special collaborations or for example worked abroad, I can say that "I worked abroad", which is a great goal that improves reputation above all. This means that we have great success and have contacted companies or people who need us in other countries, and means that we have a good knowledge of the language and the sector as we are working and relating to people who are not aware of the language we speak mainly.

Once we have understood how to find our strengths and know what they are, we have also found an activity that succeeds better than the others, which we know how to do effectively. We can make the most of this factor to dedicate ourselves further to other activities that could be useful in the future, or even to have an extra competence that we can expose to the public.

The weaknesses, on which we must work to try to fix them all, are those factors that do not benefit us, that in the eyes of the customers appear shoddy and not very effective. It is very important to identify our weaknesses because they could become instruments of advantage for the competition. For example: A customer needs to contact us for any information before making a purchase, but our chat and conversation system to contact the customer is poor and not effective. The customer then decides to abandon us and to go to the competition that may have noticed this weakness of ours and exploited it to the fullest, creating a better method of conversation, such as a live chat through the assistance and the customer.

This situation can also be used as a great advantage though! In fact, we can use the method that we have just shown you in our favor. For example: One of our competitors presents an online service that is very complex to use.

There! we can work on the simplicity of the service to ensure that a customer prefers us even for this simple factor. The SWOT analysis therefore serves to determine the strengths and weaknesses of any economic entity.

Increase visits

Open rate

Before understanding how to increase the rate of visits, we must first understand what it is, then the open rate or open rate. When we talk about open rates, we mean that percentage of people who have clicked and opened your advertising launch through certain emails that are addressed to specific people. It is therefore the relationship between emails sent and those that have actually been opened and consequently read. To monitor the open rate, it is absolutely not a problem, since sending an email addressed to a certain public, you will be presented with a delivery code, which will indicate whether our email has been opened or simply ignored; and even if this email were opened, for example, 5 times, the counting does not progress and only one and single opening is registered. Obviously we will never have an opening rate of 100%, (this would mean that if we sent 60 people each an email, all 60 have opened it, taking into consideration the content), it is practically impossible, even a 60% percentage of open rate is by no means a foregone conclusion, just think that if we sent our email to 60 people, 36 of them opened it taking into consideration the content; if we think about it a bit, it is not a number to underestimate even if we always try to aim higher than what is reported in the latest statistics, (just think that large companies usually have an open rate of 30/40%).

Obviously the higher the percentage of open rates, the greater the number of people who are interested in our proposal and consequently we will have more chances to find possible really interested customers, with a positive feedback on our activity and above all on our earnings.

Getting good results and therefore a high rate of openings is not as easy and predictable as it seems, because the key to finding an effective method is to experiment continuously with new messages, new offers and new proposals, until we find one that will bring us many people who will open our message, and consequently a large number of people potentially interested in our service. A very important thing that you should always do when we want to send an email, is to understand first of all who we want to address (as we will explain you better later, it is useless to propose bags, for example, to a completely disinterested public), and as a second step, mention the name of the recipient in any message, even if it is a company or a natural person. To mention at the beginning the name of the person to whom we are addressing, for example, is a fact that makes the customer feel important, that we took some time to write an email specifically to him; doing this we avoid making our message look like the usual spam of offers, promotions or other invasive things, it must instead be a message well structured and consciously aimed at the right person. Another determining factor is what we set at the beginning of the message, which will be what the recipient will first see as a notification, which will make him decide whether to simply click delete email or go into our campaign. It is practically a key factor to "conquer" a potential customer, to do this we must try to propose a simple, innovative and direct message in a few lines of text; just think of the usual whining message that we will never open, such as: "With us 20% discount on everything for the first month", we must try to express a concept in a "fun" way to make it attract and entice people to understand better what we are talking about, we must try to propose, not only a good offer, but also a different concept than usual. Finally it is important to choose a good timing, to understand what is the opportune moment to send a certain message to our recipient, many say that the most opportune moment to enter the scene is at the center of the day, at the center of the week. But surely sending a message at 11.00 pm, or at 6.00 am, is not really such a strategic move to use.

Aim for the right target

We have thought of everything to start a successful business, we have created a simple, fast and effective website, a good method to let us know, an effective method to provide assistance and a good service. The problem is, however, that customers continue to leave without even spending a penny, even if they prove interested (intrigued) by our offer and by what we offer. The problem where is it because we have done everything perfectly? Simple, we totally missed the target customers to advertise us. Target means target, that is to say of certain people to whom we should aim that we have the certainty that they are actually interested in our service or product; we therefore have a great chance that these visitors can be transformed into real customers. When we talk about target groups we refer instead to a group of more people with the same Interests, who have similar lifestyles or needs; we should always aim for a target group and propose and promote our advertising or our promotional message where all the advantages are listed, who we are and what we do. In order to understand who our target or target is, we need to know the visitor or client to whom we are referring, to understand what their needs and preferences are.

Everything we write in our public site or on any other tool that has the purpose of interfacing between us and the consumer, must therefore be entirely written specifically for the customer. The criteria to define one's own target are: sex, age, educational qualification, profession. This is to understand what we should propose: just think, how useless it would be to propose to a man an offer for a women's cosmetics store. We must also understand where we can promote our advertising campaign. As in the target, this too must be displayed on certain sites and not by chance; going back to the example above, surely a cosmetics shop would be better to advertise it on a site that targets women. Just think about how useless it would be to advertise a cosmetics store on a gym site, for example. The most successful advertisements are those made directly by the browser, which can be found easily around, without having to look for them at certain sites.

Copy strategy

The copy strategy is practically a document that describes all the key strategies of any advertising campaign. It has the task of providing all the information useful to an activity to undertake the road to success, in this document they are mainly described:

- The advantages of purchasing our product. Why should a customer choose our service or product? What differentiates us from others? What advantages do we offer? (For example: resistance, lightness and simplicity)
- If we keep all the promises we have presented to our conquering customers. For

example, a consumer bought our product and was disappointed with the quality of it because it is not as we described it before he made the purchase.

- How we present our product and service to the public. The presentation of a product is essential for a successful campaign, and to be able to do this, we must mainly use conversation. When we talk about conversation we don't want to give a false idea that it looks good or manipulate the customer's mind, but simply try to best expose our product by saying all the strengths it has. Like a gift box, practically. The more beautiful it is externally, the more quality the content will be and consequently the greater the satisfaction of the owner.

- Availability. Are we always available to ship and sell products or provide a specific service? Are we always available to provide customer assistance?

- Brand trust. What reputation have we created over time? Are we a valuable brand or a poor quality one?

These are some of the fundamental criteria we need to think about before starting a business.

Inactive customers

Inactive customers are all those customers who have bought from us one or more times, but who have no longer made purchases for several weeks or months. Users who have registered inactive who have signed up for our campaign are practically useless and represent an expense of time. When a customer registers, we know practically everything about him, work, hobbies and necessity if we have obviously subjected him to some previous survey. Before understanding how to reactivate a client, we need to be clear about why he switched from active to inactive; we must understand our mistakes and where we could improve in the future. The main factors are:

- The customer is no longer interested in our offer even though we have best exposed our theses and received a clear and direct message.
- The customer does not receive our messages as he never uses his e-mail box.
- The customer is not convinced of our proposal. This happens when we have not dealt well with the public and we have not transmitted our message.
- The customer is satisfied. That is when the customer no longer needs our service

because he needed this only in a certain period of the past, but now he no longer needs anything from us as we have satisfied his need. When he joined, he needed something that we successfully provided and solved the case.

To identify those people who are no longer active or who have simply stopped caring about us, we need to check who among all the newsletters we sent, discarded them or never opened them. Now we could do to make users who have stopped caring about us active again. We must start from the assumption that a user who has already

.

registered in the past, has already given us his confidence in us, and it is therefore easier to return an inactive customer, as he was in the past, than to conquer a new customer. But if our old client didn't respond even after we insisted with more than 5 newsletters, it means it's time to change group targets and ignore the past.

The main things to understand to try to reactivate customers are:

- Identify which customers have become inactive and understand why this happened.
- Try to catch the customers' attention.

- Make a proposal so revolutionary that it will immediately bring customers back.

- Wait and let it go.

These are just some of the many things you should do to try to get an inactive user back. However, if you send too many emails to people who have decided to ignore you, you only ruin your reputation; you should instead think about how to make new customers. The rate of inactive users also determines whether an advertising campaign is effectively effective, or not. In fact, the lower the percentage of inactive users, the greater our success, as most of our customers have clearly received our message.

The advertising campaign

The advertising campaign is the means by which any economic activity is exposed to the public to show the product or service that it wants to sell, to describe its quality, price and efficiency. The advertising campaign is fundamental when we talk about marketing, since it is practically considered the envelope of something, like the packaging of a gift; more beautiful is presented externally and the more chance we have of someone buying it. Before creating your own advertising campaign we must take into account the badget that we have available and we must decide to whom we want to focus and what are the objectives of our advertising campaign. To present an effective message that positively affects the customer we must:

- Express the benefits that the purchase of it will offer.
- Describe its usefulness.
- Send the price into the background, as a factor of second importance.

The advertising campaign can be one, which is repeated over time, or there may be more advertising different from each other but which have the same bases and the same intentions. Once a good advertising campaign has been established, we need to understand whether it is actually useful or not; to do this we have to go and see how many daily clicks we record.

Nowadays, however, it is quite complex to make a successful advertisement, since the client sees them all as something tiring and repetitive. Creativity and imagination are therefore fundamental factors for the creation of an effective advertising campaign since each campaign, behind the screen, has a complex history behind it. We therefore need to find and interpret our ideas in the best possible way, so that they are best understood by all consumers.

We have to decide several factors including language, for example. We can choose whether to make a serious and very professional advertisement, or whether to play a bit on the various themes to have a more confident and familiar bond with the customers. The visual language is also important, choosing a certain situation rather than another based on the context we want to propose is essential for a successful campaign. Obviously graphics, design and advertising in general must be relevant and above all consistent with what we really want to offer on the market or the service we offer.

The buying process

The buying process is practically the process that the consumer performs before getting to buy a certain product or service. This process lists all the strategies used to encourage the consumer to buy. This process is divided into several parts, including:

• Customer needs. At this stage we must interpret the customer's needs, to understand what kind of service or product we can offer. We must therefore look for the problem that the consumer intends to solve through our help. For example, our customer needs a new car, so we can offer a new car at a favorable price.

• The proposal at the right time. After the consumer has found a need, he is looking for a bargain at a low price and with immediate availability. And this is where we come into play, through an advertisement, we must propose an unmissable proposal. However, we must adapt to the economic situation of each individual customer, since before making the purchase, the customer always checks all the offers that have been proposed to him and consequently will choose the most advantageous one that best meets his needs, where he will have to spend less. .

● Customer decision. This is the penultimate step, or the one where the customer chooses what and from whom to buy.

● As the last step in the purchasing process we have the review. After the customer has made the purchase he will decide to write a review (feedback), based on how satisfied he is, whether we have interpreted and handled his problem as well as possible, or if he has been disappointed because we have not kept our promises. However, this results in a huge decrease in purification level.

In other words, the phases are: Need, Knowledge, Evaluation, Purchase, Review.

Mistakes to Avoid in Email Marketing

- ▢   Many times, when we use email to satisfy, promote an advertisement or to talk with a client, we often make several mistakes that could send us on the wrong path. The most common mistakes made by those who want to take the path of email marketing are

- ▢   Send too many emails on the same day to the same consumers. This concept applies both when we want to send more emails in the same week, as when we send a newsletter to our customers every day. All this becomes very invasive for the one

369

who receives our emails, making it him upset and he blocks all the emails we want to send him.

☐ Propose the same concept several times. This happens when we sent an email to a client and it was successful, proposing and describing our ideas or product. After we have noticed that our email was successful, we then decide to send the same email again, or by changing some terms to the same customer. It is a mistake to be avoided in order not to tire the customer and make him run away.

☐ Write to avoid appearing inactive. This happens when after sending a message that has been successful, we no longer know what kind of concept to propose or what message to send. Therefore, we decide to send superficial things and concepts that are useless. These useless messages will be immediately rejected by the recipients without even reading them.

☐ Improvise the contents of an email. When we write an email for a target, we need to know who we are targeting to understand what type of words to use and how to structure the email for each individual. Improvising at the last moment is absolutely wrong because to write an email we must first set up points to write in the email, such as: "promote a product, or provide information about what we do".

- ☐ Be in a hurry to send a message. As just mentioned, it would be advisable to write a list to be able to best send a message for the client. There is no hurry to send a message to the customer, since we have neither a deadline, nor the risk that if we do not send any email for a period of at least 7 days we will lose the customer. In short, take your time to set up a message that will work and hit where and how you want. To do this we can also use images attached, although it would be better to set your message more verbatim than by photo. The text must be useful, simple and must explain everything in the best way. A non-formal text style must be used, so we avoid using the third person as a form of courtesy. While the images must be captivating and simple, avoiding inserting too many concepts in a small space or inserting only text as nobody will read it.

The Importance of Statistics

Statistics are data collected over a specific period and route. Statistics have the task of making a person understand the various events that occurred during a predetermined period, topics such as: earnings, revenues, objectives achieved, strengths and weaknesses. A detailed analysis to draw up a list of all the statistics of your activity is usually made every weekend, at the end of the month or every year. The statistics therefore serve to determine the general situation and what has been done for a given period and aim to improve that figure for the future and how to do it. For example, this month we spent

€200,000 for various overall expenses, and we made 30 sales of € 60.00 each, with a total revenue of € 1800.00, making the difference between the revenues and the total expenses, we therefore found a gain of € 1600.00.

Next month we are aiming to make a revenue higher than the previous month to increase the sum of earnings. To do this we must either increase the sales of a product or increase the price of it. The analysis of any economic activity is expressed through graphs or tables where all the data and phenomena that occurred during a certain period are inserted and described. This analysis is fundamental to establish new objectives and to understand the mistakes we have made. Taking time and doing a detailed analysis of the statistics means not only understanding how things are proceeding and if we are reaching our goals, but also making a self-assessment. To do this we can use certain software where all sales are described, the transactions and purchases we made every day. These software systems are also able to show general activity through percentages or direct numbers, relating earnings, revenues, expenses and any losses.

We can also use this tool to identify how things are progressing individually, so for each employee in part we can monitor the work done, the time taken or the sales made; so if something doesn't work in our business we don't blame our whole team, but we can go and analyze who actually is doing their job incorrectly.

Lead Magnet: How to Attract Customers

A Lead magnet is content designed specifically for the customer. It has the task of attracting the attention of consumers and above all convincing them and encouraging them to leave their contact information, such as their email address, so that we can interact with him over time. This factor is essential when we talk about marketing, as it is the basis of 'conquering' the customer before doing anything else. There are various strategies that we can use in a Lead magnet, they can be simple or complex and the most important thing is time, and above all, knowing how to wait. To give an example of a lead magnet we propose this situation: A consumer is looking for a course on how to improve the open rate, he comes across a site where he can download the appropriate file. He must first provide his email. In this case the lead magnet is the service in exchange for the email to which we could send various offers or discounts in the future. It is therefore a content:

- Completely free of charge for those who need it
- Easily obtainable by exchanging contact information, such as e-mail

- Can be downloaded by everyone at any time

The main objective is to help us set up a list with all contacts and potential customers by choosing an appropriate target. Then in the future we could send emails to entice the purchase of the good or service we are offering. It is also useful for showing your professional image to a wide audience of people who will make a good impression of us, positively increasing our reputation, and we enter the mind of those who buy. This means that every time you think of a product that we offer, you will think of us.

Customers usually buy only from those who they trust and actually know or have already had purchased from in the past. Furthermore, this system is able to attract a large number of people, including people who are interested in buying. We then have a target to which we aim, then from there narrow to only consumers who actually intend to buy from us. The larger the number of people we are able to give us their email address, the more possibilities there are to find more potential customers and increase profits.

The Lead Magnet therefore represents the first step on the road towards the purchase.

It must be structured properly to give the impression of a serious and professional proposal. It must include content that can establish a first relationship of trust between you and the customer. They must make a transition from "I'm looking for someone to help me" to "I found the perfect person for me" only through this first step. Our main objective is that when they intend to buy, they prefer to buy with us, thinking of the competition as an alternative, uncomfortable and ineffective way. As mentioned above there are various types of free Lead Magnets that we can establish, including:

- If we offer a service or a free trial for a certain period that expires with the purchase proposal
- Discounts or with offers on the final purchase
- A video file that best describes the service or product we offer in a simple and direct way. This type of video must be short and appealing, with a nice design and must aim to show us as a trusted seller

In short, we can count on a high number of solutions. Obviously, we will choose the most appropriate and relevant one based on the service we offer.

We could do a self-assessment, thinking ... If I were in the customer's shoes, would I give my email in exchange for this service? Is it really worth it?

Now let's see how to create a Lead Magnet and what fundamental characteristics it must have to be effective and downloaded, presenting quality content. The first step in understanding how to create a quality lead magnet that is useful is to know who we are addressing and the problem or need for our product or service. For example, we know that we are turning to an online product seller, we could offer some sort of guidance on how to increase sales and customers. It is practically the same concept used by stores to attract customers. Just think: winter has begun, a clothing store has put on sale all winter clothes like jackets or sweatshirts. Surely the number of customers will increase after this strategic sale. The only difference between an online activity and the clothing store is that in the online activity the proposals are made based on the customer's knowledge, instead in the shop based on other factors.

We don't know who our customers are as we turn to a vast number of people who can buy from us and not to individual targets.

In our case knowing how to help the customer is fundamental. Among all the customer's needs we must try to satisfy the most urgent one so that he will come back to us also in the future. Before exposing a solution to a certain customer product that we found we must be clear on how we want to solve the problem. Explain step by step how to solve the problem, using terminology that is not too complex. Be direct and avoid presenting a hasty and inadequate response, take your time, reflect and be informed so that you can set up a message of success that attracts the customer. Focus on one problem and satisfy it well, remember that this is only the first step towards the customer, so you have to give a sample of your skills and of what you know how to do! The customer must quickly understand the mistakes he has made or the information he needs. If he cannot understand what you are saying as it is too long a message with complex terminology and poor design, he will surely ignore and forget about us. Since the Lead Magnet is free, we must avoid uploading and divulging too much information that could possibly be useful in the future for solving a problem.

The lead magnet, therefore, is not only a tool to attract as many customers as possible, but it is a means that should not be underestimated as it is the first step to have the customer's trust. We must express ourselves and make ourselves understood perfectly. Our only purpose is to give our customer a contact so that in the future when we send a proposal or an advertising campaign, he knows that he can trust us and that the advertising we have proposed presents a quality product or service.

New Techniques

Lead Nurturing

Lead nurturing is a marketing strategy with a main objective is to aim and ensure that we establish a conversation with the customer. This strategy does not serve to promote a product or a service such as in an advertising campaign, but is to establish and improve a direct relationship of trust and knowledge between the customer and the seller. This trust is used to have the customer to buy from the seller not only for the quality product or service he offers, but also for the relationship established between the two subjects. Doing this will also make the customer believe that the competition is an uncomfortable and unknown variant from which you should be wary. We must forget everything else and put the customer at the center of everything so we must listen to him and transmit as much trust as possible.

When we establish a direct conversation with the potential client we must communicate without being intrusive. We must be courteous and be seen as the one who can easily and simply solve all the problems that are proposed to us in a short time. We must convey credibility and trust, giving the impression of a true professional. First, we must show to the customer all things we are competent in and have knowledge of in order to aid them better, such as marketing consultancy or online sales. The consumer understands that a seller to be trusted when he not only thinks about earning and being advertised, but also thinks about his customers and the trust and esteem between the two.

But what tools are best for communicating with a potential customer?

• Social networks - Social media can be a useful tool to promote an advertising campaign but also to communicate with customers and provide useful information.

Through this means we can more easily establish a relationship of trust

- Newsletters - Newsletters like social media are not just about promoting something, but we can use newsletters to talk directly with the customer, writing a welcome message and describing the product for example

Through the lead nurturing, the customer will see us through different eyes. He will see us as a professional who cares about his customers. This tool is essential to accompany the customer towards the purchase, since we can easily provide all the information he needs or quell any doubts in a short time. Obviously, the lead nurturing is not only addressed to new customers, but also to those that have already purchased from us, to ensure that they are not lost and forgotten. Since these people have already trusted our brand at least once, it would not make sense to abandon them when we can preserve them and have more chances that they will purchase from us in the future.

Webinar: Useful Information at your Fingertips

The word "webinar" comes from the fusion of terms web and seminar. The webinar is practically a lesson or a real online course that you can safely follow online from any device that has internet access. A webinar is often accessed by registering for a specific online course that can be free or paid. A webinar is a live lesson where you discuss directly with the customer as if in school. Through a specific live chat, the client can converse freely with the one who is supporting the lesson, asking questions or clarifications using typing or directly through their voice. A presentation or lesson lasts about 1 or 2 hours. To access these live lessons we must be registered at a specific site or forum in the case of a free webinar. Obviously there are many webinars where you can participate and learn a lot of new things, but not all of them are well structured and easy to understand, and certainly paid lessons will be structured and explained better than free ones. But we must also keep in mind who is directing the webinar. Just think that quality always wins over quantity, since a concept that maybe explained in a course in 2 hours can easily be explained better in 30 minutes.

Everything depends on who we decide to buy from.

Avoid paying unnecessarily and wasting your time to access random webinars. Before buying, see if that person from whom you want to buy it has good reviews, how much they know and if they are competent in the field. Based on strengths and weaknesses you could choose courses that will help you improve in these points, thus having even if you have to spend a little, you still have a good teaching from which to understand the mistakes to avoid in the future.

If you need to buy one or more lessons online, the suggestions we offer are:

• Take notes. Surely you will not remember all the important things that have been reported to you, in fact it is essential to take notes or write down the most important things

• Request all the materials used during the live as they are an important source of knowledge and strategies. Materials such as videos, images, illustrations, statistics, etc.

The perfect trigger

Triggering means when a given action is completed, another one immediately starts countering. Trigger marketing consists in the sending of a determined message in a particular period of the year or when there is a determined period, time, an event etc. These messages arrive instantly, but only at the time set by the seller. Just imagine a trigger of a gun which is activated by itself, and therefore automatically, when a target is in view. Trigger marketing works just like that. In a given period, the message we preset is sent to certain people we have carefully selected. These messages must contain promotions for special occasions, such as: It's Valentine's Day. We have prepared 1 month before for this event, we have already talked and bought a box of chocolates from the supplier, and the only thing we have left to do is resell it all. So, we prepared our unmissable offer, the box of chocolates that usually costs € 5.00, we are selling it for € 2.50, a real bargain! The autoresponder sends the promotional message describing the product and the reduced price to our directed audience. The choice lies with the customer, whether to buy or not. This explains why when there is a day of celebration, a certain product is always offered to us by email.

The Importance of Feedback

Before understanding what feedback is, why it is needed and why it is useful, we must be clear that feedback does not serve to criticize negatively or worse, to insult a person, a product or a service. Feedback should be used to freely express one's opinion regarding a given product or service in a constructive and opportune way. Obviously I will not write under to a product that has not satisfied my requirements "it sucks", but I will have to insert a detailed and pertinent description to explain to both the seller and future buyers why we decided to leave a negative or positive review. We must then describe how we found ourselves using that particular product or service, if it actually solved our needs, its quality and if it is simple and practical to use among other things. Feedback or reviews are therefore all the information from those who have used our product or service which we receive and influence us positively or negatively. Feedback is not always the best, there is more possibility of receiving a negative review than a positive one as the one who must judge must do it sincerely, listing all the points against and points of weakness that he found in our proposal . The feedback serves to give us an idea of how we are placing ourselves on the market, to make us preform a self-assessment and understand what our strengths and weaknesses are, We can used this to understand where we can improve in order to succeed in increasing sales and quality of what we are proposing. Getting feedback from people outside our business also helps us to strengthen because of different points of view and knowledge. It would be best to get as much feedback as possible from more people to get a broad perspective on the product and allows us to focus more factors on which we should work. If you need to give feedback to a salesperson, never make a critique that you never want to receive. Don't be generic, instead explain why you decided to give ⅗ stars, for example. Never write only 2 words, but formulate a pertinent and appropriate body of text that best explains the reason for your choice. For example, we need to evaluate a wool hat and we decided to include a review of ⅘ stars, in the feedback we simply wrote "Good". It is not exactly the best. There is a difference between writing a simple "Good" and writing, for example, "Excellent material, keeping warm, just like in the description, the only problem I decided not to put 5 complete stars is because the print looks slightly ruined in a part." The feedback is not just for us to understand how our product is doing on the market, but also to other customers who are undecided whether to buy from us or not. Reviews are very important.

Disclaimer

All registered trademarks and logos mentioned in this book belong to their respective owners.

The author of this book does not claim or declare any rights to these trademarks, which are mentioned only for educational and informational purposes.

Printed in Great Britain
by Amazon